Series/Number 07-128

ANALYZING DOCUMENTARY ACCOUNTS

RANDY HODSON
The Ohio State University

SAGE PUBLICATIONS
International Educational and Professional Publisher
Thousand Oaks   London   New Delhi

For information:

SAGE Publications, Inc.
2455 Teller Road
Thousand Oaks, California 91320
E-mail: order@sagepub.com

SAGE Publications Ltd.
6 Bonhill Street
London EC2A 4PU
United Kingdom

SAGE Publications India Pvt. Ltd.
M-32 Market
Greater Kailash I
New Delhi 110 048 India

Printed in the United States of America

Library of Congress Cataloging-in-Publication Data

Hodson, Randy.
    Analyzing documentary accounts / by Randy Hodson.
        p.   cm. — (Sage university papers series. Quantitative applications in the social sciences; no. 07-128)
    Includes bibliographical references.
    ISBN 0-7619-1743-8 (pbk.: alk. paper)
    1. Social sciences—Methodology. 2. Content analysis (Communication). I. Title. II. Series. Sage University papers series. Quantitative applications in the social sciences; no. 07-128.
    H61.H633   1999
    300—dc21   99-6255

    00   01   02   03   04   05   10   9   8   7   6   5   4   3   2

Sage Production Editor: Diana E. Axelsen

When citing a university paper, please use the proper form. Remember to cite the current Sage University Paper series title and include the paper number. One of the following formats can be adapted (depending on the style manual used):

(1) HODSON, RANDY. (1999) *Analyzing Documentary Accounts.* Sage University Paper series on Quantitative Applications in the Social Sciences, 07-128. Thousand Oaks, CA: Sage.

OR

(2) Hodson, R. (1999). *Analyzing Documentary Accounts* (Sage University Paper series on Quantitative Applications in the Social Sciences, series no. 07-128). Thousand Oaks, CA: Sage.

CONTENTS

Acknowledgments   v

Series Editor's Introduction   vi

1. Introduction   1
   Documents as Data Sources   3
   Introduction to Content Analysis   5
   Ethnographies as an Example   6
   Epistemological Considerations   7
   When Is Document Analysis Appropriate?   9

2. Successful Applications and Extensions   10
   Two Foundation Projects   10
   Workplace Ethnographies   14
   Available Extensions   15

3. Selecting and Coding Documents   17
   Selecting Cases   17
   Coding the Data   23
   Coder Training   27
   Reliability Checks   29
   Subtopic Analysis   29
   Electronic Scanning and Autocoding   30

4. Analyzing Documentary Accounts   32
   Common Statistical Techniques   32
   Scales and Missing Data   41
   Statistical Inference   44
   Outliers and Deviant Cases   46
   Qualitative Comparative Analysis   47
   Qualitative Data Analysis Software   48
   Summary   49

5. Reliability and Validity   **50**
  Reliability and Bias in Coding   51
  Reliability and Bias in the Accounts   52
  An Example   54
  Additional Reliability and Bias Checks   60
  Evaluating Validity   62
  Construct Validity and Theory Development   63

6. Summary   **65**
  Why Analyze Documents?   65
  Guidelines for Implementation   67
  Strengths   68
  Limitations   71
  Contributions to Social Science Knowledge   72
  A New Window on the Social World   73

Appendix   **74**

References   **81**

About the Author   **88**

ACKNOWLEDGMENTS

Many people have contributed to the development of this monograph. I am indebted to H. Russell Bernard, Dan Clawson, Michael Lewis-Beck, and Robin Stryker for their invaluable comments on earlier drafts. I am also indebted to the staff and students of the Sociological Research Practicum at Indiana University who helped to collect the data set on organizational ethnographies that serves as an example throughout this monograph. Also, I wish to acknowledge the contributions made some two decades ago by my graduate school mentors—Ron Aminzade, Bob Hauser, and Erik Wright—who taught me the necessity of precision and clarity in research. Finally, I am grateful for the hard work and intellectual integrity of the qualitative researchers who produce the accounts that provide the ultimate data source for the methods described here.

SERIES EDITOR'S INTRODUCTION

All kinds of human behavior are observed and written about or documented. These descriptions are compiled by court reporters, teachers, journalists, office workers, police, government bureaucrats, or ethnographers, to name a few. For our purposes, ethnographers are exemplary "documentary accountants." They are scientifically trained and spend months in the field as careful observers. Suppose, to take a hypothetical example, that anthropologist Barbara Brim, knowledgeable in the Quechua language, spends 18 months studying conflict patterns in the Andean farming community of Uru and reports her observations in a 300-page research monograph. We could expect to gain considerable insight about conflict in that community from reading her rich account. However, valuable as it is, it would leave us with a central question—namely, how general are the findings? For instance, are the determinants of conflict in Uru the same elsewhere?

For the "generalization problem," endemic to this sort of research, Professor Hodson provides an original solution: Draw a random sample from the population of relevant documentary studies. Let us continue our example. Suppose the population is 200 anthropological field reports from as many South American farming communities. We could randomly sample 50 and use them as a database. The next step would be coding the several variables of theoretical value. One variable might be contact with outsiders, another respect for elders (both with categories of none, little, some, considerable). Each village would receive a score (e.g., 1, 2, 3, 4) on the variable, after analysis of the contents of its ethnography. In this way, a South American community conflict data set of 50 cases would be developed, containing measures on many variables.

These variables could of course be related quantitatively. One hypothesis might be that as contact with outsiders increases, respect for elders decreases. Say these two ordinal variables are correlated, yielding a tau-b = −.40. There appears to be a moderate negative relationship between contact with outsiders and respect for elders in these communities. The generalization, technically speaking, applies to the population of ethnographic studies of South American farm communities, not to the population of South American farm communities themselves. Professor Hodson is at pains to point out this distinction and to offer measures for assessing the extent to which the two populations are in fact alike.

In using documentary works as a data source, the strengths of qualitative and quantitative analysis can be combined. But before embarking on such research, it must be determined if the population of accounts is large enough. Some successful illustrations are the Human Relations Area Files, social movement event analysis, and workplace ethnographies. Other possibilities, from a long list enumerated in the monograph, include strike studies, biographies of political elites, and historical studies of crime. Once the researcher defines the population, great care must be taken in the sampling and coding. Here Professor Hodson provides splendid guidelines and convincing details from his own workplace investigations. He gives full attention to reliability and validity issues and shows how to begin statistical exploration once the data are assembled. Quantitative analysis of documentary accounts, an innovative idea masterfully developed in this monograph, opens up a new frontier for social science research. The many valuable qualitative studies become more valuable still.

—Michael S. Lewis-Beck
Series Editor

To Susan, for her wisdom and support

ANALYZING DOCUMENTARY ACCOUNTS

RANDY HODSON
The Ohio State University

1. INTRODUCTION

The growth of documentary accounts has produced rich, in-depth accounts of social life across a wide range of topics in the social sciences. Such accounts include ethnographies, newspaper accounts, police reports, judicial records, political party platforms, bodies of regulatory law, biographies, and historic archives of various sorts (Abbott, 1992; Aminzade, 1992; Clawson & Su, 1990; Lijphart & Crepaz, 1991; Stryker, 1996). The growth of these literatures provides opportunities to develop data sets based on the systematic coding of documentary evidence. Standard statistical techniques can then be applied to the analysis of these data sets. The systematic analysis of documentary data is rapidly becoming a major growth area in social science research.

Ethnographic accounts provide particularly rich accounts of social phenomena and will be used accordingly as a central example in this monograph. Ethnographies have gained increasing recognition and acceptance in the social sciences in recent decades. Such accounts are based on lengthy periods of observation in natural social settings. Bodies of ethnographic evidence have accumulated in several subdisciplines, including organizational studies, social movements, the study of nongovernmental organizations, party politics, elite behavior, democratization, deviance, community studies, and education.

Ethnographies are frequently used as sources of insights and new hypotheses. The in-depth descriptions they provide, however, have not typically been used as sources of data amenable to quantitative analysis and to the systematic testing and evaluation of hypotheses. The Human Relations Area Files, Gamson's (1975) analysis of the strategies of social protest, and other applications demonstrate the viability of applying quantitative methods to documentary and ethnographic accounts.

1

The purpose of this monograph is to summarize in one place the methodological tools that have been developed for the analysis of complex documentary accounts such as ethnographies. The discussion covers six major areas:

- Benefits and limitations of the quantitative analysis of bodies of documentary evidence
- Population definition and case selection guidelines
- Analysis strategies
- Reliability and validity checks
- Substantive areas in which analyzable bodies of documentary material are currently available
- The use of documentary accounts for developing new measures of important concepts and for cross-method validation of existing constructs

The material for the book is based on two major sources. First, existing methodological literatures describing the process of quantitatively analyzing documentary accounts are summarized. Second, research documents, protocols, and methodological analyses from the author's own research are used as examples. The level of presentation is accessible to both master's-level and Ph.D.-level students and to more experienced researchers. Little prior statistical background is required.

Large bodies of documentary materials, both in book and article form, have accumulated in many social science fields. These materials constitute a rich body of descriptive data potentially available for quantitative analysis. A number of important research projects have used documentary materials as databases for quantitative analysis. The goal of this monograph is to systematize the methods for compiling and analyzing these data sources and to make these methods widely available.

The standard tools of content analysis provide a starting point. Methodological extensions are needed to take advantage of the fact that documentary accounts such as ethnographies often provide in-depth descriptions of settings. Consideration must also be given to the fact that a body of ethnographic work may include a variety of different theoretical orientations.

The quantitative analysis of documentary sources should be clearly distinguished from meta-analysis, which is the analysis of effects across studies (Cook, 1992; Wolf, 1986). In contrast to meta-analysis, the methods described here use ethnographies and other documents as descriptions of settings or events as if each were a highly detailed survey instrument. The analysis strategy thus treats each ethnographic account as an in-depth description of a different setting or event and then accumulates and codes these descriptions as a data set. The commonality between meta-analysis and the quantitative analysis of ethnographies is that each builds on increasingly rich bodies of extant research. Meta-analysis analyzes the findings of quantitative research. The quantitative analysis of ethnographic accounts analyzes the rich descriptions provided by field observation.

The primary audience for this book is social science researchers and those training to be social science researchers. Both quantitatively and qualitatively oriented researchers potentially will be interested in the methods described here. The methods are principally quantitative, but the data sources are qualitative accounts. Increased cross-training in methods in social science graduate programs has made quantitative researchers more interested in qualitative methods and vice versa. The statistical requirements of the method are well within basic graduate school requirements in the social sciences, making the techniques described in this book available to all social scientists.

The motivation for developing and systematizing the methodological guidelines reported in this monograph comes from the increasing availability of large bodies of ethnographic and documentary evidence across a variety of topics and subfields in the social sciences. These accounts provide a potential gold mine of data if they are systematically compiled and coded. Many of these growing bodies of evidence represent hundreds of years of accumulated professional and Ph.D.-level effort spent in observation and writing. Most remain underused as research resources, at least in part because of a lack of guidelines and direction for applying appropriate research methods.

Documents as Data Sources

The impetus toward the systematic analysis of documentary data is supported by increased interest in the analysis of textual writings in a diversity of fields, both inside and outside the social sciences. The humanities, for instance, have become increasingly involved in textual analysis in recent years and have developed their own methods and concerns (Bernard & Ryan, 1998).

Ethnographies provide in-depth observations of social settings and thus serve as a particularly useful example of documentary accounts relevant to the social sciences. Ethnography is the scientific description of naturally occurring social situations (Lofland, 1995; Morrill & Fine, 1997). Ethnographies allow us to understand a situation as the participants themselves understand it. They are invaluable to the study of process, ambiguity, and change (Plummer, 1983). Although much debate has emerged in recent years about the ability of ethnographers and other observers to be truly objective (Denzin & Lincoln, 1994), accounts from the field provide our most intimate contact with the social world as it really exists (Lofland, 1995).

Taken alone, the analytic value of each ethnography is limited by the difficulty of distinguishing idiosyncratic aspects of a situation from aspects that may be at work across a range of situations. The systematic coding and analysis of these accounts, however, allow explicit comparisons between situations, thus overcoming this limitation. The synthesis of qualitative and quantitative approaches used in the systematic analysis of ethnographic data thus combines the benefits of in-depth observation with the rigorous use of comparisons (Weber, 1990).

The expansion of the social sciences, as well as the increasing acceptance of a diversity of research methods, has resulted in the growth of bodies of ethnographic accounts across a variety of fields. Ethnographies of urban life were first made popular in the United States by the Chicago school of sociology (Schwartzman, 1993). The anthropological tradition also has contributed to the growth of ethnography across a range of topics in modern society. History and political science offer biographies of elites and nonelites, as well as contemporary and historical community studies. The accumulation of ethnographies across time has resulted in bodies of ethnographic literature with deep roots and with an ever-growing range of contemporary offerings.

A final building block in the analysis of documents is provided by an almost universal use of computers in social science research. Graduate training in the social sciences today relies heavily on computers for writing, statistical analysis, and library research. Widespread competence in the use of computers provides a foundation for the systematic analysis of documents using quantitative methods. Cross-training in qualitative and quantitative methods is also increasingly common in graduate programs in the social sciences and has produced a generation of researchers with familiarity, competency, and interest in a range of methods and in creative approaches to research.

Ethnographic accounts take months or, more often, years to research and write. One of the strengths of the methods described here is that they build on accounts that have taken many years of professional labor to produce. The quantitative analysis of documentary accounts thus produces new knowledge in an effective manner by building on already completed observations. The more thorough use of existing ethnographic accounts may further encourage their production by increasing their value.

Ethnographers in the process of framing their studies sometimes undertake comparative analysis between cases. Such comparisons are frequently cited by ethnographers as crucial for the development of reliable and valid knowledge (Morrill & Fine, 1997). For examples of some of the best exercises in case comparison among ethnographies, see Burawoy (1979), Gouldner (1964), Noblit and Hare (1988), and Lipset, Trow, and Coleman (1956). Such explicit comparisons between cases, however, are the exception rather than the rule. Even exemplary efforts at comparative analysis are typically based on a small number of cases and may draw conclusions based on a very limited range of data (Eisenhardt, 1989, p. 540). The benefit of systematic comparisons among a larger number of ethnographies is that a much fuller range of cases can be considered.

Introduction to Content Analysis

Content analysis is a widespread technique in the social sciences (see Weber, 1990, for an overview). The heart of content analysis is the coding of material from existing sources. Content analysis spans many disciplines in the social sciences. A variety of issues in political science are frequently analyzed using content analysis, including presidential politics, leadership, and government policy (Hermann & Hagan, 1998; Lijphart & Crepaz, 1991). Indeed, there has been a sustained movement in the past 30 years in political science toward combining data on political events with data sets built around more traditional sources such as voting records, surveys, and social and economic indicators (Lijphart & Crepaz, 1991). Researchers using content analysis also have analyzed trade union constitutions and AFL-CIO convention resolutions (Cornfield & Fletcher, 1998; Stepan-Norris & Zeitlin, 1995). Speeches and press conferences, diaries, newspaper accounts, television programs, advertisements, and song lyrics are all available for content analysis. Even fiction can be systematically analyzed for content. An analysis by Griswold (1992) of Nigerian popular fiction for its meanings and contexts demonstrates the range and versatility of content analysis.

After a topic is selected and a set of relevant documents is identified and assembled, the researcher specifies a set of themes of interest. The documents are then read and coded according to these themes. For instance, the researcher might code the prevalence in the documents of certain words or certain ideas. Words, themes, and ideas can then be correlated across documents and patterns established. In classic content analysis, the number of variables coded is generally fairly small, ranging from a dozen to a few dozen items. The fairly limited range of items typically coded results from the selection of documents that are themselves often quite focused in content.

Ethnographies as an Example

Larger documentary accounts such as ethnographies provide a unique opportunity to apply content analysis techniques to professional reports entailing in-depth, detailed accounts of social situations. Such accounts differ somewhat from the traditional texts analyzed using content analysis. For one thing, they are typically longer and more detailed, thus allowing a much larger number of variables to be coded. They are also written by trained professional observers who are specialists in the topic under study. The accounts thus offer particularly rich sources of insight. The themes and content of an ethnographic account have been carefully selected to include coverage of topics of interest to researchers in an area of study.

Ethnographers and other professional observers are trained to observe systematically and to report their observations objectively. These aspects of their training further increase the value of their accounts for subsequent analysis. As trained observers of social behavior, ethnographers can provide rare in-depth reports of both social behaviors and the contexts in which these behaviors naturally occur. People who speak the language of the people whom they are studying and who have spent a considerable amount of time in the field are likely to observe and report events and situations more accurately and with greater comprehension than observers who are less deeply immersed in local realities. The analysis of ethnographies thus provides a rare opportunity to systematically compare in-depth accounts of behaviors across contexts. Ethnographers in specific substantive areas also are trained to provide observations on some minimum set of core issues important to the area. For instance, organizational ethnographers routinely provide information on work group size, coworker relations, management relations, and technology. The consistency with which core topics are covered facilitates the combining of accounts into analyzable data sets.

Social surveys also provide opportunities to compare across contexts but with some key differences. The depth of material available about the contexts of behaviors from surveys may be limited to what can be asked over the telephone using a brief and standardized set of questions. Social surveys also more commonly inquire about attitudes than about behaviors. Attitudes are easier to ask about using standardized questions, but they may not be closely related to actual behaviors because the context for attitudes is by necessity left somewhat abstract or hypothetical (Deutscher, Pestello, & Pestello, 1993).

Ethnographies and documentary accounts are thus our main source of information about behaviors in naturally occurring situations. The specific accounts reported in ethnographies are distilled observations selected by ethnographers as examples of observations occurring across a wide window of observation. As distilled accounts, based on a great range and depth of observation, they provide particularly useful data for analysis.

Ethnographic data also provide special opportunities and needs for methodological checks. The methodological variables that can be collected include the time spent in the field and the theoretical orientation of the ethnographer. These factors allow evaluation of the reliability and objectivity of the underlying accounts as well as the reliability and objectivity of the process of coding data from these accounts. The inclusion of these methodological variables allows researchers to investigate the process through which ethnographic and documentary evidence is constructed (Denzin & Lincoln, 1994). The ability to engage in systematic analysis of the construction of the underlying documentary evidence is an important bonus to the systematic study of these documents.

The coding of data from accumulated documentary accounts holds great promise for the social sciences. These observational records are rich and cover a wide range of topics. The method is cost-effective because it builds on prior research efforts. The method is also cumulative—new accounts can be added as they are produced. Ongoing projects also can be expanded to cover new topics (see Vallas, 1987).

Epistemological Considerations

The systematic analysis of documentary accounts starts with the assumption that the real world is being observed and reported. The accounts are treated as summaries of the experiences and observations of the primary observers in the field. The interpretation that the observer makes of his or her primary observations is not a focus in this usage. The view of ethnographic accounts as objective reports is consistent with classic visions of the ethnographer as a skilled and trained observer (Strauss & Corbin, 1990). The aspects of ethnographies of particular value for their use as data sources are their grounding in "deep familiarity" with local realities and "true content" (Lofland, 1995).

The systematic analysis of a body of documents, however, also allows an investigation of bias and selectivity in the reporting of observations. Chapter 5 discusses ways to evaluate the assumption of objectivity by analyzing the role of observer characteristics as biasing influences on the accounts produced.

The methods described in this monograph are based on the content analysis of a large number of case studies. Case analysis is widely employed across the social sciences. Debates among the different approaches to case analysis span disciplines ranging from history to political science to sociology (Fredrickson, 1997; McMichael, 1990; Oyen, 1990; Stevens, 1997). The unique strength of the systematic quantitative analysis of cases is that it is able to specify in detail relevant aspects of the social situation under consideration and investigate the extent to which these aspects actually covary with the behaviors of interest. Systematic quantitative analysis is also able to specify multiple causes (and to determine the weight of their relative contributions), consider interaction effects among multiple determinants, and evaluate the role of measurement error (Lieberson, 1991).

The systematic analysis of a body of ethnographic work provides an important safeguard against some of the limits of research based on analyzing just one or a few cases. An important limitation of such research is its tendency toward particularizing—toward making claims that are relevant only to the current case. Alternatively, cases are often presented as if they are widely generalizable, without evidence being presented to support their generalizability (Ragin, 1987, p. 69).

The systematic coding and analysis of data from ethnographies also highlights important questions concerning the nature of ethnographic knowledge and its sources, validity, uses, and relation to other types of scientific evidence. Can the behaviors reported in the various ethnographies be usefully reduced to a more defined set of variables? Are the findings based on such codings overly abstract, having lost relevant specifics during the coding process? Outlining procedures to safeguard against these and other possibilities is an important goal of this monograph.

When Is Document Analysis Appropriate?

Researchers should consider the analysis of documentary accounts if their primary research goals are the testing of particular hypotheses and theory verification and development. Documentary accounts provide rich descriptions of social behaviors and surrounding contexts that allow a wealth of hypotheses and theories to be tested. If a research area includes a sufficient population of existing documentary accounts, then systematically analyzing this rich body of data may well be an effective way to significantly advance knowledge in the area.

Analyzing ethnographic and documentary accounts, however, is not suggested under certain conditions. If the central concern is with some aspect of social reality that appears to have been almost entirely overlooked by prior researchers, then there is no substitute for going to the field and observing this aspect of reality directly. A thorough review of the literature, however, should be undertaken prior to reaching this conclusion. Few topics have been completely overlooked. It is more likely that their role and importance have been underrecognized or misunderstood. If this is the case, then additional observations are not necessarily the answer. Systematic analysis of the existing record of observational data may be more useful as a starting point.

Also, if the research goal is to establish, as accurately as possible, the prevalence of a commonly recognized population characteristic or phenomenon, analyzing documentary and ethnographic accounts may not be the best strategy. Census data or other data from nationally representative samples are preferable for such efforts. Ethnographies do not typically constitute a pool of observations that can be reasonably argued to be statistically representative of broader populations. Their unique contribution is in shedding light on complex phenomena and relationships that have previously gone unobserved or been misunderstood, not in establishing precise estimates of the population distributions.

In Chapter 2, some of the major projects based on the content analysis of documentary and ethnographic accounts will be examined. Chapter 2 also includes a list of research areas with large bodies of ethnographic data that have not been systematically analyzed.

Chapter 3 provides detailed information and examples on how to organize a coding project, develop the coding instrument, train coders, and develop procedures to increase reliability. This chapter describes the essential elements of the method.

Chapter 4 provides insights on how to analyze the data once they have been collected. The full range of statistical techniques is available for such analysis.

Chapter 5 presents important reliability and validity checks that can be undertaken using data from ethnographic accounts. These methodological checks are an important part of the analysis and provide unique opportunities to analyze biases that may be embodied in the ethnographies. These techniques are important for establishing the validity of findings based on the data. These checks are also useful for investigating the manner in which documentary and ethnographic accounts are socially constructed.

Chapter 6 provides a summary of the method. It identifies the key strengths and limitations of the systematic analysis of documentary accounts. It also provides a perspective on future developments in the analysis of textual documents.

2. SUCCESSFUL APPLICATIONS AND EXTENSIONS

This section will describe two highly successful applications of the systematic analysis of documentary accounts. The Human Relations Area Files in anthropology is the first. The second is the analysis of conflict events by social movements researchers. The chapter will also discuss the analysis of workplace studies as an application of the systematic analysis of documentary accounts to a contemporary research area. Substantive topic areas where the method can be fruitfully extended also will be noted and key sources listed.

Two Foundation Projects

Two areas of research have provided key groundwork leading to the development of a generalizable method of content analysis as applied to ethnographic and other documentary accounts. The first of these projects rests on a centralized archive of anthropological reports on primitive societies. The second exists as a set of diverse studies focusing on social movements and using mainly newspaper accounts of conflict events, such as demonstrations, riots, and strikes.

Anthropology's Human Relations Area Files

Working over many decades, cultural anthropologists have developed an archive of ethnographic accounts with wide public access called the Human Relations Area Files (HRAF). George Murdock initiated the archive project in 1937 at Yale University. In 1949, it was incorporated as a private nonprofit organization. The archive received early sponsorship from Yale University, the Carnegie Corporation, and several other supporting universities. The National Science Foundation, the Ford Foundation, and the U.S. State Department have provided subsequent funding.

The basic unit of analysis is whole societies (mainly primitive ones), with nearly 350 societies included in the most comprehensive file. This file contains more than 800,000 pages of text based on nearly 7,000 source documents, including books, dissertations, government reports, journal articles, and unpublished work (Levinson, 1989, p. 84).

The HRAF is a microfiche-based archive with copies in approximately 300 member libraries. The text pages are precoded and sorted by topics covered. The users of the archives must then code the variables of interest from these pages, but numerous coding projects have been published and are publicly available (Barry & Schlegel, 1980). More than 750 published articles have used the HRAF as their primary data source since it was made publicly available in 1949, including 28% published in interdisciplinary journals (Ember & Levinson, 1991).

Selected subsets of the data have been made available in recent years on CD-ROM. These subsets are topically focused, containing information on selected subjects such as human sexuality, marriage, family life, crime, childhood, socialization, education, religion, and aging.

Social Movement Event Analysis

The second set of major foundation studies for the systematic analysis of documentary accounts is a series of studies of social movements undertaken mainly by political scientists and sociologists. These projects are largely independent but have inspired a closely intertwined research tradition. In addition, the studies have developed a rigorous set of methodological checks on the data sets developed and analyzed.

The study of social movements has benefited immensely from the compilation of data from qualitative sources. Indeed, analysis of such data has provided its major empirical grounding. Gamson's (1975) seminal study of social protest used data on 53 social protest movements taken mainly from professional histories. For each social movement, Gamson coded 74 characteristics based on content analysis of movement histories (Gamson, 1975, pp. 24-25). The variables coded included violence (by or against the group), secrecy, factionalism, hierarchical versus decentralized authority, bureaucracy, alliances, social class of membership, and many other group characteristics.

More recently, social movement researchers have expanded both the types of data used and the range of topics analyzed. The focus, however, has remained on "the occurrence, timing, and sequencing of such events as regime changes, riots, revolutions, protests and the founding of social movement organizations" (Olzak, 1989, p. 119). The main source of information about social movements and social movement events has been newspaper accounts, but official archives, historical accounts, and police records also are used as data sources. For example, Tilly (1981) reports on an analysis of violent protests using French police records from 1890 to 1935. Shapiro and Markoff (1997) analyze the revolutionary demands of French citizens based on content analysis of a sample of the more than 40,000 "Statements of Grievances" sent by local political bodies to the Estates General in the revolutionary year of 1789. Television reports about demonstrations appearing on the nightly news also have provided raw data for the analysis of conflict events (McCarthy, McPhail, & Smith, 1996). Newspapers, however, remain the most widely used source of data. Newspapers have been favored because they are consistently archived, are widely accessible, and provide the most comprehensive coverage of events among available sources (Babb, 1996; Cress & Snow, 1996; Griffin, 1993; Silver, 1995; Taylor & Jodice, 1983).

The topics analyzed by social movements researchers have expanded over time to include trade union and mass strikes. Silver (1995) and others associated with the World Labor Group at Binghamton University have produced and analyzed worldwide data on the history of strikes over the past century. Their primary data sources have been reports in the *New York Times* from 1870 to 1990 and in the *London Times* from 1906 to 1990. The data coded include type of unrest (e.g., strike, general strike, riot, or demonstration), types of informal resistance (e.g., planned absenteeism), local unemployment levels, and related contextual factors.

Researchers involved in event analysis have developed detailed norms and standards for sampling accounts and for coding their contents (Cress & Snow, 1996; Olzak, 1989; Stryker, 1996). Researchers also have become increasingly sensitive to issues of reliability in coding data. Mueller (1997) compares accounts of conflict events provided by nationally circulated newspapers with those reported in local newspapers and finds that the national newspapers exhibit more ideological biases in coverage. Nationally prominent newspapers are also unlikely to report conflict events occurring in distant parts of the nation unless the events are violent or involve a large number of people. Mueller argues that for certain types of events, local newspapers may be a more reliable source of data than nationally prominent newspapers. Mueller's work is a good example of the importance of methodological investigations to the development of a research field.

The focus on newspaper archives as a primary data source for event analysis in the social movements literature allows a large number of cases to be coded but at some expense in terms of the data available about each event. For example, there are many newspaper accounts over the past 120 years about strikes, but the amount of information that can be consistently coded from these accounts is somewhat restricted. Often the coding instrument includes only a few dozen items, with many of these being not codeable from any given news account.

The focus of conflict event analysis on short newspaper accounts, however, has encouraged the use of computerized scanning technology. Such technologies can scan large numbers of newspaper articles and make them computer readable. The original goal of this research strategy was mainly to allow simple computerized searchers for key words. Recent advances in computerized language recognition, however, have allowed the development of autocoding systems that do more than just search for simple phrases and code their frequency. Such coding systems use dictionaries of synonyms and syntactic parsing (decomposition of sentences into their parts) to search and code somewhat more complex ideas (Franzosi, 1998). Event analysis has been a pivotal research field in the early application of this emerging technology in the social sciences because of its reliance on relatively short news reports and its search for data on a relatively limited set of variables. Such technologies have the possibility of greatly increasing the number of cases coded as well as the speed and flexibility of the coding process. We will return to autocoding in Chapter 3 as an area of likely future developments.

The HRAF and the content analysis projects undertaken by social movements researchers demonstrate the viability and potential contributions of the systematic content analysis of ethnographic, historical, and documentary materials for social science research. Analyzable bodies of ethnographic and documentary accounts exist for many other social science fields. We turn to organizational ethnographies as a case in point.

Workplace Ethnographies

The analysis of workplace ethnographies provides a final example of the application of content analysis to documentary accounts. Contemporary ethnographies offer accounts that are richer and more detailed than the journalistic accounts analyzed by social movement researchers and more current than those analyzed by cultural anthropologists. Workplace ethnographies provide a case in point.

Early interest in organizational ethnography in the United States began with the famous Hawthorne studies in Chicago during the 1930s (Roethlisberger & Dickson, 1939). The findings from experimental methods of studying productivity created so many anomalies that the researchers decided that direct observation was needed to sort out the complex processes involved (Schwartzman, 1993). The key conclusion from these studies was that a rich "informal culture" exists in the workplace and exerts a strong influence on productivity.

The Chicago school of sociology, with its focus on field research, also contributed to the growth of workplace ethnographies. The factory studies of the 1940s and 1950s (Dalton, 1959; Roy, 1954; Walker & Guest, 1952) combined the study of informal workplace culture with a focus on organizational characteristics and management behavior. The tradition of factory studies continues today in contemporary ethnographies of machine shops (Burawoy, 1979), longshoring (Finlay, 1988), and automobile assembly (Graham, 1995; Kamata, 1982).

White-collar workplaces became a focus in the 1960s, starting with the seminal work of Crozier (1971) on clerical work. Today, the study of white-collar organizations has developed its own traditions and interests, including a central focus on the role of bureaucracy in the workplace. Research on these issues is carried forward today in contemporary ethnographies of banking (Smith, 1990), insurance (Burris, 1983), legal offices (Pierce, 1995), engineering (Kunda, 1992), and direct sales (Biggart, 1989). The central rationale for these organizational ethnographies—both those of factories and those of office settings—is that the depth of observation afforded the ethnographer, who spends months or even years in a setting, allows greater insight into circumstances, behaviors, and meanings in a workplace than data based on surveys or company records. The latter are seen as tapping only surface attitudes or organizationally scripted facts (Schwartzman, 1993; Smith, in press).

Researchers have sometimes attempted to more fully mine the methodological potential of organizational ethnographies by systematic comparisons among limited sets of ethnographies (see, e.g., Gouldner, 1964; Homans, 1950; Lipset et al., 1956). Such efforts, however, are the exception rather than the rule and are generally quite limited in scope. As a result, the insights generated from such comparisons have been useful for generating new concepts and hypotheses (Burawoy, 1991; Feagin, Orum, & Sjoberg, 1991; Guba & Lincoln, 1994), but less progress has been made in discarding outdated ideas (see Ember & Levinson, 1991, p. 79; Naroll, Michik, & Naroll, 1980, p. 482). These comparisons are based on insufficient cases to effectively discredit even outdated ideas. The successful use of ethnographies as an effective tool for generating rich descriptions, but their limited role in theory testing, is also noted by Ragin (1987, p. 53).

As a consequence of the limited use of systematic comparisons among organizational ethnographies, the depth of observation contained in ethnographies only recently has begun to be used effectively to select among theories and thus to advance our understanding of the workplace. The loss is considerable. More than 100 book-length organizational ethnographies have been published in the English language. Each represents, on average, more than a year in the field, with at least as much additional time spent in analysis and writing. The accumulated record of organizational ethnographies is thus based on more than 200 years of Ph.D.-level observation and interpretation. But this resource has remained largely unanalyzed by social scientists studying organizations.

Only by using systematic methods of comparison among these ethnographies can we introduce the methodological tools of probabilistic (as opposed to deterministic) causality, measurement error, and multiple causation into the interpretation of ethnographic accounts (Lieberson, 1991). Examples of the application of systematic techniques to the analysis of organizational ethnographies are used in subsequent chapters to illustrate the potential research gains attainable from the analysis of documentary accounts.

Available Extensions

Rich bodies of contemporary documentary and ethnographic accounts are available on a broad range of topics of interest in the social sciences.

In an analysis of article submissions to the *Journal of Contemporary Ethnography,* Adler and Adler (1995) identify several topical areas with large numbers of submissions. These areas include occupational cultures, religious groups, cults, masculinity and femininity, sports and entertainment, education, aging, health and illness, police and courts, military, poverty, identity formation, negotiation processes, and technology.

The large number of ethnographic accounts of school desegregation, for example, makes the coding and systematic analysis of these a possibility (Noblit & Hare, 1988). Likewise, ethnographic accounts of juvenile delinquency treatment programs exist in sufficient number to be analyzable. Studies of childhood and adolescence, family relations, communities, and race and ethnic relations include similarly rich ethnographic traditions.

As already noted, the social movements literature has benefited immensely from the analysis of historical and journalistic data on social movements. In recent decades, ethnographic and documentary accounts of social movements also have accumulated. Systematic analysis of these could provide an opportunity to investigate some of the underlying process variables so important to social movement theory.

Additional areas with large bodies of documentary accounts amenable to systematic analysis include the following:

- Studies of planned organizational change and job redesign (Applebaum & Batt, 1994)
- Strike studies (Clark, 1997; Franzosi, 1995; Lendler, 1997; Zetka, 1992)
- Riots and revolutions (Gailus, 1994; Hart, 1997; Olzak, 1989; Stone, 1979)
- Community studies (Demos, 1970; Hareven, 1982; Ladurie, 1974; Lockridge, 1970; Slayton, 1986)
- Biographies and autobiographies of political elites (Edwards, Kessel, & Rockman, 1993)
- Biographies and autobiographies of nonelites (MacFarlane, 1977; Plummer, 1983, p. 15)
- Court rulings and judicial biographies (Baum, 1995; Coffin, 1994; Davis, 1989; Douglas, 1980; Gunther, 1994; O'Brien, 1997; Rothwax, 1996)
- Studies of state and community politics (Castles & Mair, 1984; Formisano, 1983; Hicks & Kenworthy, 1998; Thornton, 1978)
- Contemporary and historical studies of crime and dissidence (Roth, 1992; Shaw, 1951)

How would one find out if an area of interest has enough documentary accounts of sufficiently high quality to proceed with analysis? The answer is provided in the next chapter, which addresses the issues of identifying sources, developing coding schemes, and coding the data.

3. SELECTING AND CODING DOCUMENTS

This section describes strategies for compiling a comprehensive list of documentary accounts on a topic. Computer-aided searches are a central part of this strategy. We also discuss sampling and the conditions under which sampling is appropriate. The central focus of the chapter is on the development of coding schemes and protocols for coding the data. We describe procedures for field-testing coding instruments and for training coders and supervisors. Inference and missing data are important concerns in the coding of documentary data. Strategies for avoiding or minimizing these problems are outlined. The use of inference in assigning codes needs to be minimized. Missing data need to be coded as such, thus retaining maximum flexibility for the treatment of missing data at the analysis stage.

Selecting Cases

Having identified a research area in which there are available documentary accounts to analyze, how is one to identify and select the specific cases to analyze? The answer to this question is crucial to the project. The researcher will spend a lot of time with the accounts selected. It is important to make certain that their analysis will meet the research goals.

The theoretical goals of the study play a leading role in determining the criteria for selecting cases. The substantive knowledge of the researcher contributes to case selection through an awareness of categories of documents that do and do not fit the criteria for selection (Stryker, 1996). The researcher must develop explicit selection rules to distinguish between cases that are within the population of interest and those that are not.

An important early choice is whether to include books, articles, or both. *Book-length documentary accounts* contain a wealth of information. These accounts easily allow the coding of up to a hundred or more variables, thus allowing a wide range of subsequent analyses. Coding a reasonably large set of book-length accounts, however, is no small project. Each can take 40 or more hours of work. An initial estimate of the number of books will thus provide an estimate of the number of weeks of full-time effort required to code the data. Additional time is required for developing the instrument, keypunching the data, analysis, and so on.

Articles take less time to code but provide more limited information. If the researcher's interests in the topic are highly focused, articles may be a good choice, but the resulting data set will have a narrower range of utility. Combining books and articles is also possible. Initially, it is probably better to code one or the other and then consider whether to extend the project to include both.

Explicit criteria should be developed for accepting or rejecting a document. For instance, length of time spent in field observation is an important criterion. Professional ethnographers usually consider 6 months to be the minimum time needed to get sufficiently "behind the scenes" to record the true underlying nature of a setting. It is also important to clearly specify the substantive domain of the study. If a researcher is studying deviance, are both adult and adolescent deviance of interest? Should studies of courts and detention facilities be included as well as studies of primary deviance and deviant careers? It is important early in the process to examine a sufficient number of cases to make informed decisions about selection criteria. Make these decisions explicit and stick with them. These decisions are crucial to defining the nature, purpose, and outcome of your study.

Population Size and Sampling

How many documentary accounts are necessary to allow quantitative analysis of the resulting data? No precise answer to this question is possible. Several guidelines are possible, however. For multivariate analysis in the social sciences, at least 100 cases are generally required. Another rule of thumb is 15 cases per explanatory variable. Thus, if the intended analysis specifies 6 explanatory variables, a sample size of 100 should be sufficient. Additional controls require additional cases. Univariate and bivariate analyses can be done with as few as 40 to 50 cases. Generating the required number of cases may require that the population definition be expanded to include unpublished articles or dissertations or that the time frame covered be extended backward.

If the researcher is in the fortunate position of having too many cases to code given available resources, *sampling* techniques are appropriate. It is essential that the selection be done according to random sampling principles so that the resulting sample is statistically representative of the larger population (Kalton, 1983). Random sampling is essential so that the results from the sample can be generalized to the larger population of documents. For a detailed example of the application of sampling procedures to the selection of documentary accounts, see Gamson (1975).

Search Strategies

Major sources of information useful for locating documentary accounts include the following:

- Computerized library and journal archives
- Bound journal volumes
- Library shelves in the area of volumes already located
- Bibliographies of the accounts already located
- Compilations and archives that have already been developed on the topic of interest

Thorough knowledge of a substantive area will generally include awareness of existing sources and archives. If you do not feel deeply knowledgeable in an area, you should consult with senior scholars and library archivists in the area. This process may uncover sources that you would have never considered. Even well-informed researchers should consider checking with other knowledgeable sources as a first step in the research process.

Electronic databases of books and articles have become widely available in recent years. They also have improved in quality, comprehensiveness, and accessibility. In addition, they are rapidly being extended backwards in time to include sources from earlier decades. These databases include the Educational Resources Information Center (ERIC), *Dissertation Abstracts International,* and the Social Science Citation Index (SSCI) as well as online files of books and documents held by libraries. The SSCI is one of the best, perhaps because it is one of the most recent to become available online and therefore uses the latest and most up-to-date software and data archives. Reference librarians often have valuable inside knowledge about additional specialized citation source files. You should cross-check the key citation sources used to make sure that they are not leaving out important citations. It is essential to use multiple search strategies to ensure full coverage. A partial list of documentary accounts based on an incomplete electronic database that leaves out many accounts is not a good starting point for a lengthy research project. The target is to generate a complete list of all the accounts that meet the stated criteria. Cross-checking multiple sources is an important safeguard toward achieving this goal.

Another useful strategy for identifying documentary accounts that are published as journal articles may seem somewhat dated, but it is still highly effective. Go to the main journals that publish the accounts and look through the bound volumes. This will uncover a wealth of accounts that might otherwise be invisible because of vague titles or simply because they are outside the population included in an online archive. Social science journals that routinely publish documentary accounts include the *Journal of Contemporary Ethnography, Comparative Studies in Society and History, Social Science History, Past and Present, Human Organization, Journal of Management Studies, Social Problems, Studies in Symbolic Interaction,* and *Qualitative Sociology.* In addition, each topic area also may have one or more journals that regularly publish documentary accounts. Academic journals are increasingly becoming available online. Electronic searches of the main journals producing documentary accounts are thus increasingly possible. Edited books on special topics are another rich source of published accounts.

Searching the library shelves in the immediate vicinity of volumes already located is also an effective strategy. Many accounts can be uncovered in this way that you might otherwise never find. The reason that this strategy is an important supplement to electronic searches is that key word searching is a very inexact process. Searching the shelves is also an absolute necessity if the target population includes books that are published prior to the most recent decades. (Electronic databases typically include only the most recent decades.) Even the process of searching the nearby library shelves, however, can be electronically assisted. A first pass at this project generally can be done at the computer—most library search routines have an option for viewing the titles of adjacent volumes on the shelf through scrolling backward and forward. At some point in the process, however, there is no substitute for hands-on visual scanning of a shelf of books or an edited volume of articles.

As the search proceeds, additional tools become available. The bibliographies of the works already identified provide an important source of additional citations to examine. Examining bibliographies helps the search reach backward in time. To search for current releases, publishers' lists can be an important tool. The publication of studies on particular topics may be a special focus for a publisher. Thus, it is often possible to identify the main publishing house (or houses) for accounts on the topic of interest. Examining publishers' lists of current and new releases can uncover accounts that are too new to be electronically listed or that are not yet released. The process of developing the initial list should thus be an iterative one based on using several different methods.

As the list develops, the researcher engages in an initial selection process based on the fit of the document, book, or article to the selection criteria. Accounts that pass this *initial selection* stage are then available for a more thorough screening. It is important to separate this *final screening* from the initial selection process (Gamson, 1975). Having a final screening as a separate stage allows the researcher to apply the selection criteria in a more consistent and rigorous fashion. This final screening is important for producing a list of cases that fits the population of interest as closely as possible. Application of the final selection criteria in a happenstance, changing, or variable fashion during the search and identification stage can result in the inclusion of cases with a poor fit or in the exclusion of cases with a good fit.

It also may be worthwhile to include unpublished accounts. Unpublished dissertations provide a large body of unanalyzed book-length accounts. *Dissertation Abstracts International* provides a relatively complete listing of dissertations. Conference papers provide a large body of unanalyzed article-length accounts. These unpublished papers can be accessed by looking through the proceedings of the annual meetings of the relevant professional associations for recent years. In addition, each topic area may have a special repository of published and unpublished holdings. For instance, the Harvard University Business School library has a large repository of documentary accounts of business organizations (Harvard University, 1998).

An Example

Strategies for identifying and selecting appropriate documentary accounts can be illustrated by considering the search procedures employed by Hodson, Welsh, Rieble, Jamison, and Creighton (1993) for generating a pool of workplace ethnographies. Only book-length ethnographies were considered because the topics of interest included worker citizenship and resistance, management behavior, and organizational characteristics—topics not consistently covered in depth by shorter article-length accounts of workplaces.

Many thousands of case studies were examined in a two-phase procedure to locate appropriate book-length ethnographies. First, likely titles were generated by computer-assisted searches of archives, by perusal of the bibliographies of ethnographies already located, and by a search of the library shelves in the immediate area of previously identified ethnographies. We screened titles using online computer archives, book reviews, or direct examination of the books selected from the shelves. Repeated application of these procedures constitutes what we believe was an exhaustive search—eventually our pursuit of new leads produced only titles already considered. We excluded cases that used primarily archival or survey data for their analysis rather than ethnographic observation. This selection process yielded a pool of 365 books as potential candidates for inclusion.

During the second phase of selection, we examined each book directly. The criteria for inclusion were (a) the book had to be based on direct ethnographic methods of observation over a period of at least 6 months, (b) the observations had to be in a single organization, and (c) the book had to focus on at least one clearly identified group of workers—an assembly line, a typing pool, a task group, or some other identifiable work group. The requirements of an ethnographic method and a focus on a specific work group were necessary to limit the pool to cases with the depth of observation needed to reliably ascertain the various facets of workplace relations of interest. The focus on a single organization was necessary to produce measures of the organizational characteristics that we hypothesized to be key determinants of workplace relations.

Of the 365 books, 86 were retained as appropriate for analysis and 279 were rejected. Of those rejected, more than 200 were excluded because they reported on an occupation as a whole rather than on a particular group of workers in a specific organization. These studies generally failed to provide reliable measures of either work group relations or their organizational correlates. About 25 books were excluded because they studied industries rather than specific organizations. These studies also generally lacked good firsthand information on worker relations. Fifteen books met the three criteria for inclusion but were either so short or so loosely written that accurate or complete information could not be ascertained. Thirteen books were excluded because they focused primarily on a specific job redesign program. Again, these books did not provide adequate information to code many of the variables in which we were interested. Eleven books were community studies, often of a factory town. These studies were typically based on observing and interviewing people and families outside of work and not inside the workplace. As a result, these books generally failed to provide adequate organizational or labor process information. Eight books were excluded because they focused on a particular strike or collective action and included little material on the nature of work or the labor process. Six books were excluded because they concerned plant closings and the resulting stresses and dislocations. These books also provided little material on the nature of work or on workplace relations prior to the shutdown. Seven books were rejected because they were company histories or executive biographies and contained little information on the actual work taking place in the organization.

In all cases, we examined each book carefully to see if it met the three criteria for inclusion. In some cases, a book was relatively weak on one criterion, but the depth of its material in other areas allowed its inclusion. Thus, we sometimes included a book with a fairly broad occupational focus if it had excellent ethnographic material on the organization and the labor process in several occupations. For example, a book might contain information about both assembly workers and machinists. When coding material from such a book, we determined which occupational category was the major focus and coded only material about that occupation. In some books, the data allowed the coding of two cases. For example, we coded two cases from a book reporting on a cocktail lounge—one for waitresses and one for managers (see Spradley & Mann, 1975). Gouldner's (1964) *Patterns of Industrial Bureaucracy* also generated two cases—one for underground miners and one for workers in the gypsum board factory. We coded multiple cases from 10 books. We included books based on observations of several organizations if descriptions of the labor process were particularly strong. Such books were included only if the organizations were similar and were discussed in detail. We coded organizational characteristics for these cases from a composite.

Application of the above criteria generated 108 cases from the 86 published ethnographies. We believe these cases constitute the population of book-length English-language ethnographies that provide relatively complete information on a single workplace and on an identifiable work group within that workplace.

Coding the Data

Collecting original data is generally a highly rewarding experience for researchers. It is also a lot of work, so it is important that this work be done right. The researcher may be analyzing the data and writing papers from it for years to come. Decisions made at the point of data collection have lasting consequences. A systematic approach to developing a data collection instrument is the key to success.

The Coding Instrument

The first step in preparing a good coding instrument is to survey thoroughly the existing literature on the topic being studied. List the major concepts appearing in that literature. These are the concepts that you need to include in the data collection instrument. If a concept is complex and has several facets, make sure that you include all facets. In addition, the accounts may allow the coding of topics and issues that are not routinely analyzed in the published research record. A good familiarity with the published literature may suggest some of these areas. For instance, do the accounts allow the coding of more in-depth information on the behavioral settings than is typically available in survey-based investigations?

If book-length accounts are being coded, the coding instrument can be quite long, perhaps containing as many as 100 to 200 variables. In surveys, the need to maintain respondent cooperation limits the effective length of the survey instrument. Coding documentary accounts avoids this limiting factor. The limiting factor for documentary accounts is the ability of coders to keep in mind the various variables they need to code as they read the account. If the coding instrument is too lengthy, coders may not recognize a passage as containing the answer to a question on the instrument because they have forgotten it. Periodic review of the instrument at the end of each chapter will help limit this problem. Documentary accounts are rich sources of data. The best advice is to generate a relatively complete instrument and then develop procedures to ensure that it is filled out as completely as possible. It is also important for the coder to record the page numbers on which the information leading to each code is to be found. The coding instrument for the project using workplace ethnographies described in this monograph is provided in the appendix as an example (see also Hodson, 1996).

After the initial instrument is developed, it must be field-tested on a set of accounts. This process should not be skipped over or abbreviated. It is important to test and refine the questions and the answer options in an interactive process with the data to be coded. This process may entail the reading of a half dozen or more complete books or even more articles. During this time, the researcher also will be making decisions about which questions to code as open-ended responses and which to code as fixed-option responses. Open-ended responses will entail additional work at the data analysis stage but may be important for preserving complete information where a given question has a wide range of answers (see Tilly, 1981, pp. 76-79).

The code sheet contains the questions and the answer options. Additional decision rules also may be developed about how to interpret certain types of passages. These rules are important for establishing consistent criteria for coding the accounts. These rules need to be put in writing and compiled into a supplemental *coding protocol* that is reviewed regularly. Coding protocols should be developed as fully as possible before the start of the major data collection stage. Later revisions are also typically necessary, especially in the early stages of the coding process. These protocols will be essential during the analysis stage as aids in remembering how specific variables were coded. Detailed protocols are invaluable if the data set is shared with others who were not involved in the initial data collection process.

Methodological checks are a final category of variable to include in the instrument. These checks include information both about the documentary accounts and about the coding process. Information about the documentary accounts is easy to record and can and should be recorded at the data collection stage. Methodological variables about ethnographic accounts might include the following:

- How long the ethnographer was in the field
- Page length of the ethnography
- Year of the observations
- Training of the ethnographer
- Observational role taken by the ethnographer
- Types of informants used
- Theoretical orientation of the ethnographer
- The ethnographer's organizing question

These questions will potentially be very useful in later analysis for establishing the presence or absence of bias in the accounts. Analysis of these methodological features can provide valuable insights about the accounts as a data source. Such variables also can be invaluable for studies of the social construction of the information embodied in the accounts. It is thus crucial to include the appropriate methodological variables in the coding instrument.

Information about the coding process also should be recorded. What are the demographic characteristics of the coders, such as age, sex, and ethnicity? At what stage or date in the coding process was the account coded? The analysis of methods checks on the documentary accounts and on the coding process will be the focus in Chapter 5, which is on reliability and validity.

Avoiding Inference

The consistent coding of a phenomenon by different coders is essential for reliability. Coding documentary accounts requires intellectual engagement with the written text, and the coding of many variables requires some interpretation of the text (Stryker, 1996). If substantial inference is required, however, different coders may arrive at different codings depending on their possibly divergent assumptions. Excessive inference erodes reliability.

The main way to limit the need for inference is to develop and code concepts that are not highly abstract. For instance, Tilly (1981, pp. 74-75) contrasts the reliability of two questions—one abstract and the other more concrete. The concrete question is the occupation of the social group engaged in a strike. Answers to this question were coded with high reliability (94% consistency between pairs of coders). The other question concerned the degree of coordination of the strike as a whole. This question requires considerable judgment and interpretation. What exactly constitutes coordination? How much preplanning does the concept of coordination imply? For a variable meant to distinguish between coordinated and spontaneous disturbances, Tilly found only 22 agreements out of 37 possible pairs of independent codings (59% consistency). Tilly notes that the underlying concept of coordination requires the synthesis of diverse bits of information and is quite abstract, making it difficult to code reliably.

The researcher may be very interested in a somewhat abstract concept, such as the level of coordination of strike activities. However, in the coding phase, such concepts need to be disaggregated into simpler components that can be reliably coded. In the current example, these components may include such items as the presence of leadership, evidence of prior meetings to establish a plan of action, use of social control within the group, and so on. During the analysis stage, these components can be reassembled to measure the concept of coordination in its various facets. In this way, required inferences can be made explicit and are under the control of the researcher.

Missing data is a particular challenge when coding documentary accounts. Some accounts may not address issues that are included in the coding instrument. Missing data will be especially problematic when coding articles, which are more limited in scope than books. Again, inference should be avoided. If a phenomenon is not discussed, it should not be coded as absent. For example, the absence of a discussion of accidents and injuries at a workplace should not be taken as evidence of a safe workplace. The ethnographer may simply have considered this a peripheral topic and not discussed it. Accidents and injuries should thus be coded as missing in this case. If, in the analysis stage, researchers want to infer the absence of the phenomenon, they can do so. Such inference might be based on the values of other variables that were coded and that provide some basis for the inference. By avoiding inference at the data collection stage, researchers do not lose the ability to infer based on reasonable assumptions. Rather, they delay the process and make the standards of inference consistent and explicit. Where there is substantial missing data on an important variable, especially if it is the dependent variable, the only appropriate solution may be to analyze only those cases with data present.

Coder Training

Coder training is an important part of any research project. Few faculty researchers will have the time to code all their own data. Grant support should be sought if at all possible. Even small amounts of internal support can greatly facilitate a research project. In the absence of support, sometimes a graduate seminar can be arranged so that part of the course work is to code one or more books.

If the primary researcher is a graduate student, hiring additional coders may not be within the project budget. Even in this case, however, it is important to have at least some cases duplicate coded by a student colleague to check reliability. Such help might be arranged as part of an exchange of labor among peers in a graduate cohort. Using multiple coders not only lessens the work of the principal investigator but also allows important reliability and bias checks on the data-coding process.

Coding documentary accounts makes high demands on coders' comprehension. "Text coding beyond simple words requires text understanding; text understanding involves complex linguistic operations affected by the reader's knowledge, both general and specific, and by the reader's capacity to memorize and recall information" (Franzosi, 1990, p. 451). These demands are increased by the lengthy coding instruments used for documentary accounts, especially for book-length accounts. The good news, of course, is that longer accounts allow the coding of more information than shorter accounts. Shorter accounts are easier to code but may lead to more missing data. They may also encourage a greater use of inference in coding variables because of the more limited information available (Weber, 1990, p. 40).

To ensure data quality, it is important to select, train, and supervise coders carefully. For the workplace ethnography project by Hodson et al. (1993), the book-length ethnographies were read and coded by a team of four researchers (the principal investigator, a project director, and two senior graduate students) and by eight members of a graduate research practicum. All coders were trained on a common ethnography and met twice weekly as a group to discuss problems and questions. Coders recorded up to three page numbers identifying the passages used for coding each variable. We instructed coders to look for behavioral indicators or specific descriptions for each variable coded and not to rely on the ethnographers' summary statements or evaluations (Weber, 1990).

The coders were allowed to select which books they wanted to read and code to optimize their motivation for reading the books carefully. Greater interest may increase the care with which coders read the accounts and may result in better-quality data being recorded (Franzosi, 1990, p. 453). As a result of the decision to allow coders to select books from the pool based on their own preferences, however, any "coder effects" in the data are open to multiple interpretations. Coder effects could result either from coder bias or from the unique characteristics of the subsample of books that each coder selected.

We used missing value codes where there was insufficient information to code a variable, and no attempt was made to use proxy indicators at the data collection stage. We also avoided making any assumption that the absence of discussion about a given aspect of work constituted evidence of the absence of the phenomenon itself. If information on a certain feature of the workplace was not provided, the corresponding variable was simply coded as missing. Most organizational ethnographies discuss a core set of topics, but each ethnography has areas of greater or lesser coverage.

It is also important to debrief the coders and review their codings in detail after every case is coded. This requires a substantial time commitment on the part of the principal investigator or project director. Such debriefings, however, are essential for catching coding errors and for ongoing training and quality control. Debriefing is essential for maintaining consistent coding procedures between coders and across time. For the workplace ethnography project, coders were debriefed by a member of the research staff after completing each book to check the accuracy of their codings. At this time, all codings were reviewed in detail.

Reliability Checks

Duplicate coding should be built into the coding process to allow the reliability of the data-coding process to be evaluated. If these checks are evaluated on an ongoing basis, they can also help identify questions in need of refinement or coders in need of greater training or closer supervision.

A good rule of thumb is to have at least a 10% sample of the cases coded by a second reviewer (Elder, Pavalko, & Clipp, 1993). Once a coding operation is in place and functioning, a 10% increase in the number of cases to be coded translates into a relatively small allocation of resources, many of which have already been expended in the process of initiating the project, developing the coding instrument, and selecting and training coders. The additional resources allocated to duplicate coding will be well spent. Without reliability checks, the researcher has little information about the quality of the data. If the researcher has built reliability checks into the data collection process, then an informed discussion of the quality of the data becomes possible. The quality of the final cleaned data set also can be improved by averaging the two sets of codings or by reconciling discrepancies by returning to the primary data.

Errors can also creep into data through keypunching mistakes and clerical errors. Errors of this sort further erode the reliability of the data. Fortunately, such errors are relatively easy to identify and correct. Data can be double punched and the files compared to ensure an exact match. Variable frequencies can be examined to locate codes outside allowable ranges. Variables can be cross-tabulated and inconsistencies investigated. These checks are easy to implement using standard data analysis programs and should be pursued rigorously (Franzosi, 1999).

Subtopic Analysis

Additional topics can be analyzed by focusing on subsets of accounts or by coding additional variables for a topic of special interest. For example, researchers using the Human Relations Area Files have initiated a number of projects in which subsamples of cases with data on special topics are further investigated. These projects include studies of child rearing and time allocation (Munroe & Munroe, 1991).

Using organizational ethnographies, race relations at work could be further analyzed by coding additional concepts for the subset of ethnographies that describe organizations with racially mixed workforces. Similarly, additional variables could be coded for the subset of organizational ethnographies that describe gender-mixed workforces, perhaps focusing on coworker relations or related topics (see Welsh, 1994).

One of the benefits of ethnographies is that they often report the history of events leading to a current situation. Recent developments in sequence analysis allow the identification and comparison of complex causal paths from event histories such as those available in documentary accounts (Abbott & Hrycak, 1990; Griffin, 1993). Such causal sequences can be investigated by coding data from the documents for important types of events and event sequences.

Electronic Scanning and Autocoding

Recent advances in technology have created new opportunities for social scientists interested in the analysis of textual data. Electronic scanning, for instance, has become more reliable and cost-effective. Scanning allows large bodies of textual data to be rendered available for computer-assisted coding.

These new computer-assisted technologies make the free searching of large amounts of textual material for ideas and concepts much easier and much less tedious than searching by hand. The limitation of these methods is that not all episodes relevant to a given concept are likely to be discussed using the same words or phrases. Rigorous use of lists of synonyms and key phrases, however, can result in relatively complete searches. These technologies make extensions of the analysis to new topics and concepts less prohibitive in terms of time and effort because the entire document does not have to be reread to search for a new idea. The reduced cost of duplicating data held in such mediums also increases the accessibility of the accumulated documentary record on a topic (see Levinson, 1989).

It is also possible to code somewhat more complex concepts by using autocoding software that "interprets" passages and generates data based on the interpreted meaning of the passage (Bernard & Ryan, 1998). Researchers involved in the study of conflict events have most extensively developed such procedures.

An example of this technique is provided by Bond, Jenkins, Taylor, and Schock (1997, p. 563). For this research project, news headlines were analyzed by a software program developed to look for the following information: "Who is doing what to whom, when, where, why, and how?" Answers to each of these five questions are sought in a data set composed of news headlines and first lines of articles. For instance, the following headline was autocoded: "Eight students were arrested today by local police in front of the U.S. Embassy in Seoul after they staged a teach-in directed against U.S. trade policies." The autocoding program coded two events from this headline: (a) South Korean police arrest students and (b) students demonstrate against U.S. Embassy. The computer produces this coding by matching the words in the text against lists of acceptable words measuring each concept.

Autocoding (in combination with text scanning) allows the coding of relatively simple ideas from large numbers of cases, potentially reaching into the thousands. In addition, the coding is completely consistent in the sense that the computer will code the data the same way each time the program runs. Comparisons with human coders suggest similar or higher reliability for autocoding programs (Bond et al., 1997, pp. 567-569). An additional strength of autocoding systems is that changes can be made to the system, such as adding new codes, and the program can be rerun. Thus, as the researchers perfect the system, they can upgrade the resulting data set. Such recoding would be prohibitively expensive if done by hand.

Autocoding has two major limitations. First, autocoding is useful only for relatively simple coding projects. Thus, a software program can be developed to code five variables from the headlines and first lines of newspaper articles about conflict events. These data points can later be augmented by other data about the newspaper such as the date, city of origin, and ideological orientation of the newspaper. But the resulting data sets are much more limited than the full range of data available from extended documentary accounts. The central strength of documentary accounts, which is their depth of observation, is thus, as yet, largely inaccessible through autocoding systems.

Autocoding is a relatively new technology in the researcher's toolkit, and it is difficult to predict its range of utility. Autocoding has already been used successfully in coding conflict events. Its introduction into the coding of documentary accounts will in all likelihood be relatively slow because of the difficulty of developing software to code large numbers of complex events and relationships, especially where these are described in varying and diverse ways. Autocoding might make its initial contributions to the coding of documentary accounts in the analysis of relatively focused subtopics such as coworker relations as reported in workplace ethnographies or specific types of crime as reported in juvenile delinquency studies.

4. ANALYZING DOCUMENTARY ACCOUNTS

This chapter provides suggestions about the types of quantitative analyses appropriate for analyzing data from documentary accounts. We also discuss the use of scales for minimizing the effects of missing data. In addition to commonly used quantitative techniques, qualitative comparative techniques and other comparative strategies are also appropriate. The use of quoted material from the ethnographic accounts also is discussed as a means of returning some of the original richness of the data to the analysis.

Common Statistical Techniques

The strength of quantitative analysis is its ability to model and test associations, specify multiple causes and interactions, and evaluate these models across a range of settings (Lieberson, 1991; Ragin, 1987). Indeed, the motivation behind coding documentary accounts is the ability to use the tools of quantitative analysis on the resulting data. The full array of statistical techniques can be used with the resulting data. Such techniques range from simple cross-tabulations and differences of means tests to multivariate regression, factor analysis, and LISREL analysis of unobserved variables. In this chapter, examples of the application of some of these techniques to the analysis of data from documentary accounts will be presented. Technical discussion of these techniques is beyond the scope of this monograph. Such discussions are presented elsewhere in this series as well as in numerous textbooks.

Bivariate

The following example illustrates the use of bivariate statistics using data from documentary accounts. Worker solidarity has been a much discussed but little researched topic in quantitative analyses of the workplace. The reason solidarity has been slighted in quantitative studies is because solidarity has a significant behavioral component that is difficult to measure across settings using survey questions about attitudes. To address this problem, Hodson et al. (1993) studied the relationship between

TABLE 4.1

Distribution of Worker Solidarity by Autonomy and
Team Organization, Workplace Ethnographies (N = 108)

Variable	Little	Some	Considerable	High	Total	Number of Organizations
			Solidarity (%)			
Worker autonomy (χ^2 = 18.06, p = .114)						
None	23.1	38.5	38.5	0.0	100	13
Little	20.0	30.0	43.3	6.7	100	30
Average	15.0	30.0	55.0	0.0	100	20
High	0.0	33.3	38.9	27.8	100	18
Very high	11.1	33.3	44.4	11.1	100	9
Total	14.4	32.2	44.4	8.9	100	90
Team organization (χ^2 = 14.16, p = .003)						
No	17.9	35.9	46.2	0.0	100	39
Yes	4.9	29.3	46.3	19.5	100	41
Total	11.3	32.5	46.3	10.0	100	80

SOURCE: Adapted from Hodson et al. (1993).

solidarity, worker autonomy, and team organization using the population of English-language workplace ethnographies. Theoretical arguments and anecdotal evidence suggested that worker solidarity can be undermined by worker autonomy and by new production systems based on team organization.

We measured solidarity along five behavioral facets suggested by ethnographic studies of the workplace: cohesion, mutual defense, group leadership, enforcement of a group normative structure, and existence of identifiable group boundaries. These facets were combined into a scale of solidarity that was subsequently divided into four levels ranging from little to high (see Table 4.1). Autonomy indicates the level of worker control over task organization and was coded in five levels. Team organization refers to whether work tasks are allocated to individuals or to teams. Team organization was coded as present or absent.

Table 4.1 evaluates the relationships between worker solidarity, autonomy, and team organization. The cross-tabulation of solidarity and autonomy reveals that levels of autonomy are unrelated to solidarity. Team organization, however, is significantly related to worker solidarity. But this association is in the opposite direction of that expected—teams are associated with greater solidarity. These results lead us to conclude that prior insights suggesting a negative association between teams, autonomy, and worker solidarity were mistaken.

Multivariate

The use of multivariate techniques with data from documentary accounts also can be illustrated with an example from the study of organizational ethnographies. Hodson (1996) uses organizational ethnographies to study the consequences for workers of the increasing use of participative forms of management. This study also illustrates the use of quoted material from the original ethnographies to give greater depth to the statistical results.

Researchers view participative management as a profound challenge to traditional organizations of work, although interpretations vary concerning the direction of its impact. Some researchers view participative management as providing an opportunity for workers to exercise increased power based on heightened responsibilities. Other researchers view participative management as management's latest strategy to extract not only labor but also the knowledge of production from workers. Hodson (1996) evaluates a model of workplace organizations to examine workers' experiences of alienation and freedom across different systems of production, including those based on participative management.

Table 4.2 reports results from the regression of four characteristics of work on five forms of work organization (Model 1). Each of the regressions is statistically significant. The coefficients in these equations form a pattern very reminiscent of Blauner's (1964) finding of a U-shaped pattern of first declining and then rising satisfaction and freedom at work across types of work organization (see Figure 4.1). In the analysis presented by Hodson (1996), however, higher levels of job satisfaction, pride, and insider knowledge are reached under craft production than under participative management. Thus, the pattern is better characterized as a "backward-J" pattern than as a true U-shaped pattern. The level of effort exerted by workers exhibits the same falling then rising pattern that characterizes other worker experiences, but the level of effort under worker participation is actually higher than under craft systems of work.

Model 2 adds the mediating variables of skill and autonomy to Model 1. Skill and autonomy have positive and generally significant effects on all four facets of work. When skill and autonomy are introduced in Model 2, the effects of the five forms of work organization generally are reduced, but many effects remain significant. Thus, part of the effect of forms of work organization on the four work characteristics appears to be indirect.

TABLE 4.2
Work Characteristics Regressed on Workplace Organization, Workplace Ethnographies (N = 108)

| | Dependent Variables | | | | | | | |
| | Job Satisfaction | | Pride | | Insider Knowledge | | Effort Bargain | |
Independent Variables	Model 1	Model 2	Model 1	Model 2	Model 1	Model 2	Model 1	Model 2
Forms of workplace organization								
Craft	.571*	.175	.582***	.367**	.248	.129	.068	-.077
Direct supervision	-.350	-.045	-.266	-.081	-.208	-.055	-.235	-.227
Assembly line	-.311	.152	-.110	.184	-.318	-.048	-.110	.061
Bureaucratic	-.175	-.333	-.129	-.241*	.335*	.215	-.036	-.096
Worker participation	.276*	.153	.236**	.158*	.184*	.115	.201*	.155
Mediating variables								
Skill	—	.317*	—	.281**	—	.435***	—	.139
Autonomy	—	.343***	—	.160*	—	.011	—	.253
Constant	2.630	1.165	1.881	.965	3.460	2.650	2.137	1.599
R^2	.244***	.431***	.347***	.486***	.218***	.330***	.148**	.218***
Number of cases	101	101	100	100	92	92	95	95

SOURCE: Adapted from Hodson (1996).
*$p \le .05$; **$p \le .01$; ***$p \le .001$ (two-tailed t tests).

36

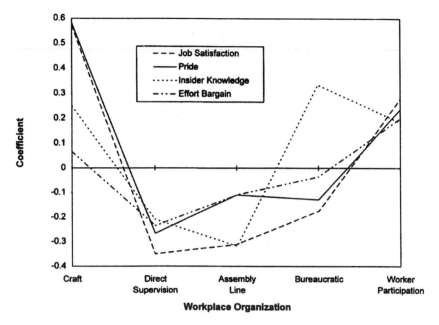

Figure 4.1. Work Characteristics Regressed on Workplace Organization
SOURCE: Adapted from Hodson (1996).
NOTE: Coefficients are from Model 1 of Table 4.2.

These effects are significantly mediated by the different levels of skill and autonomy of workers under different organizations of work.

To better understand the meaning of these statistical patterns, we can examine passages from the ethnographies that describe the situations giving rise to these findings. The following passage from an ethnography of construction work illustrates the positive association between craft organization and job satisfaction:

> Part of the culture of construction is the satisfaction of . . . winning out over the elements and showing persistence in the face of adversity. . . . Construction workers enjoy the challenge of difficult tasks and the satisfaction that comes from doing a difficult job well. (Applebaum, 1981, p. 109)

Direct supervision, in contrast to the craft organization of production, is associated with the lowest levels of job satisfaction, pride, and effort. These negative effects are even stronger than those for assembly-line work. An example from an ethnography of a plant producing processed food items illustrates the corrosive effects of direct personal supervision on job satisfaction:

> The stewards felt that the overwhelming majority of the problems that they had to deal with on their section were related either to speed-up or "the blue-eye system," the favoritism practiced by foremen in allocating the work and overtime or in moving men from one section to another. (Beynon & Blackburn, 1972, p. 145)

Assembly-line work also has negative effects on all four aspects of work studied, although these negative effects are not on average as large as those for direct supervision. Only for insider knowledge is the negative effect of assembly-line organization greater than that of direct supervision. An eloquent statement describing the nature of assembly-line work is provided by an ethnographer working as a participant-observer in a pickle plant who sees little if any accumulated knowledge in his daily tasks:

> Watching all this shiny automation carry away my laboriously lifted netfuls, I am reminded of the old cartoon of the fancy car with its hood up, and instead of an engine inside it has a cage of squirrels with a treadmill. (Turner, 1980, p. 14)

Bureaucratic organizations of work also are associated with relatively low levels of job satisfaction, pride, and effort, although these negative effects are not generally as large as those for direct supervision or assembly-line organizations of work. In contrast to its negative effect on most aspects of work, however, bureaucracy has a positive effect on insider knowledge. Workers in large bureaucracies appear to gain valuable knowledge over time about how to navigate the demands of the job. Kanter (1977) explains how this can occur in a large and highly bureaucratic organization:

> The secretarial job thus rested on a *personal set of procedures and understandings* carved out by secretary and boss. . . . The secretary/boss relation was defined *largely* by the special relationship developed by two particular individuals. (pp. 80-81)

These personal relations are one type of localized knowledge that emerges in many bureaucracies to circumvent more rule-driven methods of operation.

Finally, the effects of worker participation on all four facets of work studied are consistently positive and significant. Some of the settings with high levels of worker participation are worker-owned companies. These settings in particular evidence high levels of pride and effort. A study of plywood cooperatives illustrates these relationships:

> Ownership and participation in the co-ops also fosters an extremely strong sense of collective responsibility and mutuality. . . . "It's altogether different here [than in my former job]. . . . Here you get in and do anything to help. Everybody pitches in and helps. The people stick together, that's the reason we've gone so far and production is so high, cuz everybody works together." (Greenberg, 1986, p. 38)

As the following example illustrates, however, ethnographers are sometimes less than sanguine about the positive effects of increased worker participation:

> People are willing to put up with a great deal for this type of work. They will defend it by attacking fellow workers and by justifying outrageous abuses of power by management. . . . One male worker, a strong union activist, knew why the union had a rough time organizing at Ethicon. He knew why workers fluctuated, to the very end, between voting for or against the union. . . . "Working at Ethicon," he said, "is the best and the worst you can imagine." (Grenier, 1988, p. 32)

These results provide partial support for Blauner's (1964) U-shaped curve of declining then increasing self-actualization under modern forms of production. Under participative organizations of work, however, positive and meaningful experiences in the workplace do not return to the same levels that they achieved under the craft organization of work. This incomplete recovery of the positive experiences of craft production leaves at least some room for less optimistic visions of emergent workplace relations.

An additional example of the use of ethnographic accounts to analyze workplace issues is reported in Hodson (1995). Here the research question is whether mixed-race workforces undermine worker solidarity and the ability of workers to collectively challenge management. The results provide little support for the theory that greater minority presence in a

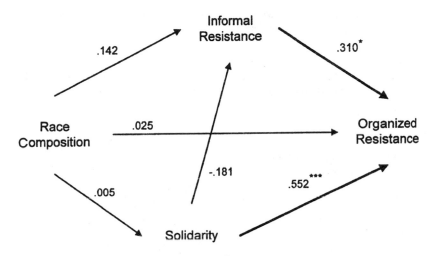

Figure 4.2. Path Model of Worker Resistance and Racial Composition
SOURCE: Adapted from Hodson (1995).
$*p \leq .05; **p \leq .01; ***p \leq .001$ (two-tailed t tests).

workforce undermines worker solidarity or hinders informal or formal resistance to management.

Figure 4.2 presents the principal findings in the form of a path diagram. Note that the coefficients for race composition are the smallest effects presented. The two statistically significant effects are those measuring the positive influences of solidarity and informal resistance on levels of organized resistance. Again, meaning and depth can be added to the statistical findings by the use of quotations.

Workplaces with low or high proportions of minority workers provide evidence of worker solidarity with nearly equal frequency. In a predominantly white underground coal mine, for example, group solidarity was pervasive. Worker solidarity in this mine extended to risking one's life for one's buddies. The ethnographer reports the following episode in which a lead worker is surveying his men who have assembled at the head of a shaft to search for coworkers trapped by a fire:

Suddenly Jimmie Isom picks up a mask from the jeep. "Put one on me, Dan," Jimmie says. Dan stares at his friend, with the deep-etched lines from his heart attack. Dan usually works Jimmie on the outside crew these days, afraid of working him inside. Now Jimmie is volunteering to go into the smoke. Dan doesn't know how to turn him down. (Vecsey, 1974, p. 190)

High levels of worker solidarity, however, also are noted in a racially diverse tuna fishing fleet, the labor force of which is composed of 40% Portuguese, 30% Mexican, 20% Italian, and 10% Anglo, Slavic, and other ethnic groups:

> Where crew members have no kinsmen in their crew, a substitute familial role identification appears to take place in stable crew settings. This seems to be a reasonable correlate of the tendency to view the ship as "home" [and includes] the desire to conduct operations in a cooperative egalitarian atmosphere with minimal clashes over decisions and authority. (Orbach, 1977, p. 168)

Informal resistance to management also is evidenced with relatively equal regularity in workplaces with high or low proportions of minority workers. For example, branch managers in a large and predominantly white banking company refused to go along with top management's agenda of deceiving workers about upcoming layoffs and instead developed agendas that were more in keeping with the interests of their workers. These agendas included being open about the pressures for layoffs from top management while organizing the workers to increase productivity and simultaneously pressuring top management to maintain full staffing levels (Smith, 1990, pp. 104-108).

Workers in a racially mixed garment factory, however, also evidenced strong collective forms of informal resistance to management. Following the delivery of a new baby garment to be sewn, the ethnically diverse female workforce spontaneously resisted because of the unacceptably low piece rate attached to the work:

> "Every time the minutes are given they get worse, they want more from us every time. Well it won't work. I can't do that target." . . . Some sat defiantly with arms folded while others talked together in small groups. The unit had disintegrated. . . . Gillian [the supervisor] was looking distraught and said: "I hate this minutes thing; it's the worst part of my job. I feel sick, I've got a headache." . . . Lisa, the assistant supervisor, was also looking very worried as the fury from the women grew. (Westwood, 1982, p. 51)

The results presented in Figure 4.2 also indicate that informal resistance is an important foundation for organized acts of resistance. The following series of events occurred at an apparel factory where a supervisor accused a worker of missewing garments. The episode starts with the following confrontation between a supervisor and a senior worker:

> If you continue to treat us like animals you will find your work in this factory becoming very difficult. We are not animals to be treated without any respect. We are human beings. I have been a tailor with Narayan Bros. for over seven years and have never during this time sewn short trousers like that pair we are talking about now. (Kapferer, 1972, p. 243)

As the confrontation progressed, other tailors gathered around and began chanting derogatory names at the offending supervisor, who quickly exited the line to avoid a confrontation.

Scales and Missing Data

Reliability is important for meaningful statistical analysis. Reliability is the consistency of data that are generated by repeated measurements of a phenomenon. If concepts are measured with low reliability, relationships between concepts will appear as reduced, absent, or statistically insignificant when the true problem is lack of reliable measurement. Reliable measurement of concepts is thus paramount for accurate findings and for the advancement of knowledge about a research topic. The keys to reliability are careful definition of concepts, clear coding protocol, and careful collection and checking of data (see Chapter 3). Following the careful collection and cleaning of data, the researcher can further increase reliability through the use of summary scales of key concepts.

Data from documentary accounts are well suited to constructing scales of underlying concepts because the richness of the data allows the various facets of key concepts to be measured. The use of scales increases the reliability of measurement because, by averaging a set of indicators of a concept, the underlying common element in the measures takes precedence over unreliability in any individual measure (McIver & Carmines, 1981).

Scale construction typically involves two steps. First, the available items are factor analyzed. If the items form a single principal dimension, then scaling proceeds (Dunteman, 1989). If they do not, then items are eliminated until the remaining items represent a single underlying dimension. Second, the reliability of the scale is evaluated, typically using Cronbach's alpha. Acceptable levels of reliability vary somewhat between research areas based on what is realistic given the types of concepts and measures used. However, a good rule of thumb for an acceptable alpha is .70. Scales

TABLE 4.3

Scale Construction, Workplace Ethnographies ($N = 108$)

Scales and Variables	Communality[b]	Scale Construction[a]	
		Number of Data Points Present	Number of Cases
Well-run workplace (1st eigenvalue = 2.20; 2nd eigenvalue = .80; alpha = .72)			
Organization of production	.69	4	70
Organizational communication	.46	3	27
Leadership	.66	2	9
Repair	.39	1	2
		0[c]	0
Organizational citizenship (1st eigenvalue = 3.35; 2nd eigenvalue = 1.06; alpha = .81)			
Enthusiasm	.48	7	55
Extra effort	.37	6	14
Cooperation	.58	5	19
Commitment	.40	4	4
Work avoidance (r)[d]	.43	3	7
Reticence (r)[d]	.62	2	6
Social sabotage (r)[d]	.46	1	2
		0[c]	1
Solidarity (1st eigenvalue = 2.45; 2nd eigenvalue = .70; alpha = .78)			
Mutual defense	.65	4	60
Discipline	.65	3	19
Cohesion	.55	2	11
Leadership	.60	1	7
		0[c]	11

SOURCE: Adapted from Hodson (1998).

a. The two right-hand columns describe the number of cases that have various levels of data present for each scale. The scales were constructed by standardizing and summing the variables to be scaled and dividing the result by the number of data points present.

b. Communalities are based on a one-factor solution for each scale.

c. Scale missing.

d. r = reverse coding.

with lower alpha values can be used, but such measures are relatively unreliable and, as a result, the relationships of the scale with other variables will be reduced. Higher reliability is attained by adding measures that are highly correlated or by increasing the number of measures used (if they are reasonably highly correlated).

The construction of a set of scales using data from organizational ethnographies is illustrated in Table 4.3. The table reports the alpha reliability and the first and second eigenvalues from the factor analysis. The communality is the correlation of the measure with the underlying scale and shows which measures are most centrally related to the scale. The communalities can help the researcher interpret the relationship of the scale to its various components. Thus, for the scale measuring "well-run workplace," the organization of production is more central than the level of repair or organizational communication.

Missing data can be a problem for researchers, and data based on documentary accounts are not exempt from this problem. Indeed, to the extent that accounts are partial in their coverage of topics, missing data can be a serious problem. One way to lessen the problem of missing data is to use scales that use all the data that are available. Such scales will have a value for every case for which data are available on any of the component variables.

Table 4.3 illustrates the use of scales to lessen the impact of missing data. The two right-hand columns describe the scale construction process. The scale is constructed by standardizing the components, adding them together, and dividing the sum by the number of data points available for each case. (The standardized components also can be weighted by their factor loadings prior to summing, but this is optional.) The resulting scale has a value in each case for which data are present for any of its components. The extreme right-hand column reports the number of cases that have each level of data present. A missing value indicator is assigned to cases with no data present. This procedure is preferable to computing a scale only for those cases with full data present and then designating other cases as missing because it retains the full information that is available for each case.

Missing data for concepts measured by a single indicator can be handled by imputing values based on the values of related variables that are reported in the data set (Rubin, 1987). For example, suppose a researcher is interested in analyzing organizational commitment, but commitment is missing in some cases. Organizational commitment can be predicted from job satisfaction, and the predicted values can be used to replace missing values for organizational commitment. As with scale construction, this technique makes maximum use of available information.

Analyzing only those cases with full data present is another solution to the problem of missing data. This solution, however, may not be realistic for multivariate analysis based on data sets with average to substantial missing data. Selecting cases with all data present for all variables can restrict the cases analyzed to a small and unrepresentative portion of the population or sample. When selecting a set of cases based on the presence of data, it is thus best only to select on data present for the dependent variable. Scaling or imputation is a preferred technique for handling missing data for the independent variables. Researchers also can consider statistical program options to assign mean values to missing cases or to analyze the data based on *pairwise presence* of data if scaling or imputation is not a viable option.

Statistical Inference

Statistical inference is the science of estimating whether an observed relationship in a data set really exists or if it occurs as a result of chance. An observed relationship might occur by chance because the set of cases randomly selected is not representative of the larger population. Larger samples greatly reduce the likelihood of such occurrences and are thus preferred. Statistical inference is an important tool in evaluating observed findings and is appropriate when the researcher has drawn a random sample from the larger population.

If the researchers have uncovered, to the best of their abilities, all the documentary accounts on a particular topic, then they will be analyzing the *population* of such accounts, not a random sample from that population. In such cases, coefficients describing relationships between variables (mean differences, correlations, regression slopes, etc.) are the exact calculations of the relationships that actually exist in the population under consideration, assuming no measurement error. The coefficients have no random component based on variability introduced by the chance draw of a random sample from the population. In this situation, tests of statistical significance are neither necessary nor appropriate.

What broader population do the documentary accounts on a particular topic represent? And how is the researcher to generalize to that broader population? The available documentary accounts on a topic typically cannot be considered a random sample of the larger population of all cases of the phenomenon. Each was undertaken by a separate researcher who selected the case based on some combination of theoretical interest and access. As a result, the researcher can reasonably argue only that statistical relationships uncovered represent the phenomenon as it is reported in available accounts. The researcher may also be able to argue, based on supporting evidence, that these accounts are representative of the broader population of interest. Such claims can be bolstered by comparisons showing similar distributions of key characteristics in the documentary accounts and in the larger population represented by these accounts. Such distributions might be generated from the census or from other comprehensive or representative sources.

Statistical inference, however, is not directly relevant to establishing the generalizability of findings based on the analysis of documentary accounts to the extent that these accounts are not based on random draws from a broader population. Statistical inference provides little guidance in situations in which the cases are not randomly selected from a larger population. Tests of statistical significance can still be calculated and are still reported by statistical analysis programs. But these tests cannot be interpreted as indicating a given probability that the relationship occurs in the broader population.

If the researcher selects a random sample of documentary accounts, then statistical inference is helpful for establishing that the relationships observed in the sample generalize to the population of all documentary accounts of the phenomenon. However, this still leaves unanswered the question of the relationship between the population of documentary accounts and the broader population of all cases of the phenomenon.

The researcher must proceed carefully then in making generalizations based on the analysis of data from documentary accounts. Statements about the generalizability of the findings should be made cautiously. Statements that specific relationships are observed in documentary accounts are appropriate. However, generalizations to the broader population must be supported by a discussion of the relationship of the documentary accounts to the larger population of interest and cannot be made on the basis of statistical inference alone. Additional support for the credibility of findings can be established by demonstrating that theoretically known relationships are observed in the data and at similar magnitudes to their levels observed in other settings.

Should the researcher even bother to present tests of statistical significance under these circumstances? The answer is a qualified yes. Tests of statistical significance can help provide a standard of comparison to discuss which effects and relationships are of greater magnitude than others. Statistical tests are also so much a part of the expected standards of evidence in social science writing that reviewers and readers of the research will be confused and somewhat at a loss without them and are likely to demand them, even when they are not entirely appropriate. The best solution is to present such tests but to add a caution that they are not sufficient to establish the generalizability of the results. Evidence on the relationship of the documentary accounts to the broader population of interest can then be provided to evaluate the generalizability of the results.

Recently developed techniques called *bootstrapping* allow the estimation of the sampling distribution of statistics on the basis of repeated draws from a set of existing cases (Mooney & Duval, 1993). These inferential techniques for estimating standard errors are an alternative to assuming random sampling and a normal distribution of test statistics. Bootstrapping techniques allow the calculation of standard errors for statistics from complex samples of the sort represented by multistage probability sampling designs. These techniques offer an additional partial solution to the problem of estimating statistical confidence intervals for complex samples. Such techniques, however, do not automatically overcome the problem of generalizability associated with nonrandom samples. Such issues are best addressed by explicitly comparing sample characteristics with the characteristics of the broader population.

Outliers and Deviant Cases

Data sets based on documentary accounts will tend to be small to average in size. Several additional statistical considerations are suggested by the relatively small size of these data sets.

Statistical coefficients sometimes can be altered by the inclusion of a few cases that are extreme outliers. In data analyses based on relatively small numbers of cases, outlier effects can be particularly strong. Researchers using data sets based on documentary accounts may want to consider eliminating extreme outliers and then reestimating the coefficients. In general, only cases more than two to three standard deviations from the mean are considered outliers. If coefficients are relatively stable between the full and reduced data sets, then the researcher can consider the results robust. If the coefficients differ dramatically, the coefficients based on the reduced data set generally will be considered the more reliable estimates of the true effects. Comparing coefficients across various definitions of the sample to be analyzed is just one technique within a larger set of strategies called *sensitivity analysis*. Other types of sensitivity analysis involve adjustments in the model or in the transformations of the analysis variables (Cohen & Cohen, 1983, pp. 286-287).

Deviant case analysis addresses related but distinct problems. Some cases may evidence relationships between variables that are different or even opposite those theoretically expected. Cases with high values, under conditions in which low values are expected, are called deviant cases. Researchers can isolate these cases and look in more detail at their characteristics in an effort to discover what produces the seeming anomaly. What is distinct about these cases that might suggest an explanation? Deviant case analysis offers potentially rich rewards through the discovery of patterns of multicausality and parallel causality and through the discovery of functional equivalents and intervening variables (Naroll et al., 1980, p. 513; Ragin & Becker, 1992).

Deviant case analysis is a technique used by both quantitative and qualitative researchers (see Noblit & Hare, 1988). It is a strategy thus especially well suited to the statistical analysis of documentary accounts because of the merger of qualitative and quantitative techniques in this method. Statistical techniques can reveal outliers and deviant cases. Computer searches can locate the exact cases involved, and reexamination of the qualitative data can provide the sort of in-depth information needed to generate new insights about the processes involved.

Qualitative Comparative Analysis

Qualitative comparative analysis uses Boolean algebra as an analytic tool to systematize comparisons among cases (Ragin, 1987). Boolean algebra defines outcome states in terms of the presence or absence of a series of characteristics. Cases are first characterized in terms of yes/no variables along a number of dimensions considered important to a particular outcome of interest. The various patterns among the explanatory variables are then analyzed in the search for the most common patterns leading to the outcome. Researchers can effectively investigate complex patterns of *conjunctural causation* using qualitative comparative analysis.

The method is particularly well suited to the sort of medium-sized data sets characteristic of documentary accounts. To use this technique with an existing data set, the researcher simply conceptualizes relevant variables in binary terms and recodes the data accordingly.

The central strength of the method is its ability to model complex interactions in terms of distinct patterns among the explanatory variables. The ability to model these complex, conjunctural patterns of causality allows a focus on cases as more holistic accounts and combines some of the strengths of case analysis and quantitative analysis (Ragin, Mayer, & Drass, 1984). The technique is thus particularly well suited to the analysis of ethnographic and other documentary accounts that build on those same strengths.

Qualitative Data Analysis Software

Computerized qualitative data analysis programs have become increasingly popular in recent years (Burgess, 1995; Dohan & Sanchez-Jankowski, 1998). These programs may or may not be particularly useful for the analysis of sets of documentary accounts of the sort discussed in this monograph, depending on the goals of the analysis.

Computerized qualitative analysis programs do not transform qualitative data into quantitative data for statistical analysis—instead, they leave the data in their original qualitative form. The programs allow the marking of passages in the original textual data as representative of certain concepts or ideas. Researchers can then pull these passages together for easy comparison and analysis. Subsequently, as researchers begin to perceive subcategories within the phenomenon or to suspect relationships between phenomena, they can specify such relationships, and the computer will sort similarly coded passages into subcategories or array passages together that exhibit the suspected connection.

Computerized qualitative data analysis programs are most useful as a tool for analyzing data within one qualitative project toward the goal of category specification and theory development. They are less useful for the goal of theory testing. Theory testing has not been a central orientation in qualitative analysis, and the programs are less oriented toward this goal than toward theory development.

Qualitative data analysis programs, however, may have a future role in the analysis of archives of documentary accounts. If the body of documentary accounts can be electronically scanned and each one treated as a "respondent" within one large case, then qualitative programs might be useful in analyzing the resulting body of data.

Significant technical, legal, and resource hurdles would have to be overcome along the way, however. The accounts may simply be too long to analyze effectively if left in their original qualitative form. The project of scanning even a moderately sized pool of documentary accounts would require significant time and effort. The process of cleaning and editing the scanned data would, in all likelihood, be even larger. Fifty accounts of 250 pages each represents 12,500 pages to be scanned and edited in preparation for analysis. The legality of fully scanning a copyrighted book, even for research purposes, is also questionable. Documents in the public record, however, such as court rulings and the *Congressional Record,* are unprotected by copyright restrictions and, in general, can be legally copied and scanned.

Coding textual passages in terms of qualitative concepts requires careful reading. This process is equivalent to the work of reading and coding the documentary accounts for quantitative analysis. For qualitative analysis, however, the reading continues to the next stage as the researcher rereads similarly categorized passages and develops subcategories and hypothesizes relationships. This iterative project would entail successive rereadings of selected components of the accounts. As a consequence, qualitative analysis programs are somewhat constrained by the demands of analyzing data in their original qualitative form to analyze only a relatively small number of cases. This analysis strategy thus loses many of the benefits of systematic controls and the analysis of multiple patterns of causality, which are strengths of quantitative analysis based on a large number of cases.

Nevertheless, there may well be a role for qualitative analysis of archives of documentary accounts. Such analysis will have to be of a smaller number of cases. In essence, such analysis constitutes computer-assisted reconsideration of the qualitative accounts as reported in the original documents. Some of the most popular programs are ATLAS, The Ethnograph, and NUDIST (Richards & Richards, 1994, p. 461). The systematic use of such programs may be able to uncover relationships and produce insights beyond those offered by the original observer, although the work required will be considerable (Bernard & Ryan, 1998, p. 623).

Summary

Researchers can use the full range of statistical techniques to analyze data derived from documentary accounts. Techniques ranging from simple cross-tabulations and chi-square statistics to the most complex multivariate statistics all can be used. However, statistical inference should be used only cautiously. The population of documentary accounts cannot generally be considered a random sample of the broader population of interest. In this situation, generalizability is argued by demonstrating the comparability between the documentary accounts and the broader population across relevant dimensions. New techniques outside traditional statistical measures, such as techniques based on Boolean algebra, are also appropriate and should be considered.

5. RELIABILITY AND VALIDITY

Reliable and valid data are essential for the advancement of knowledge. The quantitative analysis of documentary accounts lends itself well to the analysis of the reliability and validity of both the coding process and the underlying data. Reliability and validity studies by researchers engaged in the systematic analysis of documentary accounts often will be the first systematic studies of the reliability and validity of the documentary accounts being analyzed. These studies thus have important methodological contributions to make to the field beyond the specifics of the substantive issues being studied.

Documentary accounts are not randomly occurring events, and professional observers are not blank slates waiting to be written on by respondents and informants (Guba & Lincoln, 1994). Researchers must thus consider the possibility of biases in the selection of sites by the primary observers. Observers pick sites that match their substantive and theoretical interests (as well as on the basis of access and convenience). Primary observers also may be selective in their observations, interpretations, and reporting of events.

Reliability in documentary accounts can be evaluated by considering the time spent in the field, the page length of accounts, the number of words or pages given to different topics, and the use of substantiating evidence. *Bias* in the data can be evaluated by examining the effects of theoretical orientations and originating questions.

The coders who read the documentary accounts also may have biases based on their own theoretical orientations or backgrounds. Coding protocols and training may not overcome these biases completely. Techniques for increasing reliability need to be built into the data-coding process through the development of clear coding protocols and through the training and supervision of coders (see Chapter 3). The researcher will need to have included repeat codings for at least some cases to evaluate the reliability of the coding process.

The validity of concepts can be established by cross-methods comparisons between the techniques described in this monograph and other quantitative and qualitative techniques. Some of the greatest benefits of the quantitative analysis of documents lie in its ability to contribute to the construct validity of concepts through the interactive refinement of these concepts over time.

Reliability and Bias in Coding

Most of the work to increase reliability will have been completed in the data collection stage of the project. Once the data have been collected, the level of reliability of the data has been set. During the analysis stage, however, researchers can determine the level of reliability of the coding operation. In so doing, researchers provide important information for themselves and their readers about the nature of the data. Analyses of reliability also contribute to the development of the storehouse of knowledge about how to collect reliable data.

Reliability can be evaluated by using either of two calculations: intercoder correlations and intercoder agreement. Both calculations depend on having used multiple coders to code at least some cases. *Correlations* between the scores of coders who have coded the same data can be used as a measure of reliability. This strategy was used by Hodson (1998) to evaluate the reliability of the coding of workplace ethnographies. One book was selected as a reliability check and coded independently by three reviewers. The correlations between these different codings indicate a relatively high degree of reliability (average intercorrelation = .79). An alternative approach to calculating intercoder correlations uses the codings of two or more coders across a larger number of cases but for one variable. The latter strategy produces a reliability coefficient for the coding of that particular variable. The former strategy evaluates the coding process as a whole.

The *percentage of intercoder agreement* between two or more coders can be calculated by cross-tabulating their codings and counting agreements versus disagreements. Cook (1992, p. 304) reports the percentage of agreements for variables based on content analysis ranging from 56% to 100%. Tilly (1981, p. 74) reports the percentage of agreements ranging from 59% for more abstract variables to 94% for more concrete variables, again highlighting the importance of developing concepts and coding procedures that are as clear and specific as possible.

A *kappa statistic* measuring level of agreement also can be calculated. The kappa statistic standardizes the percentage of agreements on the number of categories and on the marginal distribution of responses to adjust for chance agreements (see Elder et al., 1993, for an example).

Coder bias also can be evaluated. Data on coders are easy to collect, but the opportunity often is overlooked by researchers consumed with the details of the coding operation and with the substantive questions being studied. A code identifying the specific person who coded each case should be included in the instrument. Additional information of potential importance includes the coders' sex, age, education, race or ethnicity, area of training, and other characteristics that may influence their codings.

Finally, much learning and some fatigue occur during the process of a coding project. It is thus important to record the date on which a given account is coded. This information can later be used to check for any secular trends in the data that may have occurred during the coding project.

Reliability and Bias in the Accounts

Just as reliability and bias in the coding process can be investigated, so too can researchers investigate reliability and bias in the documentary accounts. These investigations can shed important light on the nature of the observational method as it has been applied to the research area under investigation.

Several options are available for handling *differential reliability* across the documentary accounts. These options include stratifying the data into subsets with greater and lesser reliability for subsequent analysis and weighting the cases by various measures of reliability.

Sources of greater or lesser reliability in documentary data include the following:

- Time spent in the field
- Use of multiple data sources
- Explicitness of descriptions
- Page length of accounts

Probably the most important indicator of the reliability of documentary accounts is the amount of time the researcher spends in the field. Six months to a year is typically considered the minimum necessary for gaining an adequate understanding of a setting (Naroll et al., 1980). Anthropologists have long understood that a reasonably long stay in the field is essential to accurate understanding. Bernard (1988, p. 468), for example, reports on an analysis that found an unexpected negative relationship between societal complexity and female status. When the analysis was restricted to cases in which the observer had spent at least a year in the field, the observed relationship reversed and was consistent with theory and prior observations.

The use of multiple data sources and the types of data sources used are also important components of reliability in documentary accounts. Are additional supporting documents considered, such as company records, police accounts, local surveys, or school records? How many people did the observer speak with in depth? Was the range of contacts wide or narrow?

The explicitness of the descriptions provided in a documentary account also can be used as a measure of reliability. Does the observer speak only in abstractions and generalities? Or does the observer give detailed and specific examples of behaviors and also make informed observations on their prevalence? Anthropologists using the Human Relations Area Files (HRAF) consider the explicitness of accounts an important indicator of overall data quality and frequently include it as a data quality control measure (Naroll, 1960).

Other characteristics of documentary accounts also can be used as indicators of the quality of the data. The page length of the account is an important indicator of the depth of the observations involved. Page length can be used either as a weighting factor or as a basis for stratifying the cases for subsequent analysis. The number of page sources for a key variable can be taken as an indicator of the reliability of that particular variable. The number of data points present for scale computation for each case can be used in a similar manner. An aggregate count of page sources recorded for all the variables in the model can be used as an indicator of the overall data quality of the account.

The analysis of potential bias in documentary accounts allows the researcher the opportunity to offer valuable observations about the quality of the body of observational work available on the topic being studied. The results can be either positive or negative, but either way, they are likely to be of interest to other researchers.

Sources of possible bias in the documentary accounts include the following:

- Theoretical orientation
- Observer's role and training
- Nature of informants
- Sex of the observer
- Date of the observations

The theoretical orientation of the observer is an obvious potential influence on the content of the account. Is the observer a functionalist? A conflict theorist? A feminist? A symbolic interactionist? The focus of the account is also important. Is the study a broad consideration of the topic, or does it focus on some specific aspect? For instance, does a study of teenage life focus primarily on peer relations while another focuses on alcohol and drug abuse?

The observer's role and training may also potentially influence the observations reported. Is the observer an active participant or a passive observer? Is the observer academically trained, a journalist, or simply a group member who has decided to write about the life of the group? The HRAF uses a coding system ranging from A to Z to describe observer training and background. The codes include government official, missionary, humanist, explorer, tourist, propagandist (coded together with political scientist), educator, and sociologist (Lagace, 1974, p. 20).

The informants used can also influence the content and tone of a documentary account. What was the position of informants in the local setting? Were they powerful figures? Disenfranchised outcasts? Activists? The specifics of how to code the positions of informants will vary with the topic area, but the issue remains the same—how, if at all, might the social positions of key informants influence the content of the account?

Other obvious characteristics of potential interest include the sex of the observer and the date of the observations. The latter is essential for investigating the possibility of secular trends in the phenomenon being studied.

These features of the documentary accounts can all be evaluated as sources of potential bias in the accounts. They can also be used to stratify the cases into subgroups for further analysis. The analysis of both reliability and bias in the accounts depends, however, on having recorded the relevant variables during the data collection stage.

An Example

An analysis of the potential effects of bias in organizational ethnographies and in the process of coding these ethnographies is presented by Hodson (1998). Potential biasing effects are evaluated net of a baseline substantive model predicting experiences at work. Consequently, any observed methods effects can be interpreted primarily as indicating bias rather than selectivity. For example, if ethnographers identified with the human relations (sociotechnical) theory of the workplace find more peer training than other ethnographers, this could simply be because ethnographers interested in the human relations theory selected sites with more peer training to study this phenomenon. However, if such a relationship is evident when controlling for a baseline model that predicts peer training, then bias would be suggested. For such an effect to occur, the human relations theorists would have to report greater peer training than the level of peer training typically reported in similar settings.

Five characteristics of the ethnographies were evaluated: geographic location of the site, the ethnographer's role in the workplace, the ethnographer's theoretical orientation, the amount of time spent in field observation, and the year in which the field observation was completed. (For a similar list of methodological checks for analyzing potential bias in juvenile delinquency treatment program evaluations, see Cook, 1992, p. 101.) Three characteristics of the coding process were evaluated: the specific coder, the debriefer, and the stage at which the ethnography was coded during the project.

Equations were estimated using only those cases with data present for the dependent variable. Missing data on independent variables were replaced with mean values. Tests of significance are reported at the .01, .05, .10, and .20 levels. These generous levels of significance are used because of the small sample size, which is generally less than 100, and because of the importance of looking closely for any possible methods effects. Note that tests of statistical significance should be interpreted as suggestive only. The analysis is based on the existing population of ethnographic case studies of the workplace, and these cases do not constitute a representative sample of all workplaces.

Model 1 of Table 5.1 reports the regressions of three aspects of worklife on a baseline model of organizational characteristics. Note that the explained variance for each equation is significant at the .01 level. However, these substantive relationships, although important, are not central to our current concern, which focuses on the methods checks themselves.

The methods variables concerning the ethnographies and the coding process are entered in Model 2. Each equation remains statistically significant at the .01 level. The increases in explained variance between Models 1 and 2 for the three aspects of work, however, are only marginally significant at the .10 or .20 levels. Most of the effects are associated with the ethnographies rather than the coding process variables.

TABLE 5.1

Job-Related Measures Regressed on Organizational Characteristics and Methods Variables, Organizational Ethnographies

Independent Variables	Pride		Organizational Citizenship		Good Relations With Management	
	(1)	(2)	(1)	(2)	(1)	(2)
Organizational model						
Well-run workplace	.217****	.170***	.483****	.475****	.379****	.395****
Job autonomy	.247****	.212****	.217****	.284****	−.092	−.001
Craft organization	.406****	.524****	.127	.259	−.424**	−.456*
Injuries	−.048	.033	−.078	−.048	−.123	−.040
Ethnography characteristics						
Location						
British Commonwealth		−.384***		−.303*		
Europe		−.492***				
Third World				−.578*		
Ethnographer's role						
Observer only		−.298*				
Participant observer		−.321*		−.437*		
Theory						
Functionalist		.470**		.525*		
Human relations						
Marxist						
Feminist				.561**		
Time in field				−.027**		−.052****
Year of study						
Coding process characteristics						
Coders						
Coder 1						−1.605***
Coder 2						
Coder 3						
Coder 4						
Coder 5						
Coder 6						
Coder 7						
Coder 8						
Coder 9						
Coder 10						
Coder 11						
Debriefers						
Debriefer 1						
Debriefer 2		.637****				
Joint		.594**				
Date coded						.007***
Constant	1.500****	3.096	−.488**	−12.896	.631**	−11.358
R^2	.506****	.676****	.427****	.609****	.167****	.478****
Increment to R^2		.171*		.182*		.311**
N	100	100	107	107	100	100

SOURCE: Adapted from Hodson (1998).

NOTE: For the methods variables, only coefficients significant at the .20 level or greater are reported. The omitted categories for each variable group are as follows: location (United States), ethnographer's role (miscellaneous), theory (miscellaneous), coder (principal investigator [PI]), and debriefer (PI).

*$p \leq .20$; **$p \leq .10$; ***$p \leq .05$; ****$p \leq .01$ (two-tailed t tests).

Given the large number of coefficients estimated to evaluate the methods effects, it is important to compare the number of significant coefficients with the number that would occur by chance. For the ethnography characteristics, there are 33 coefficients (11 for each dependent variable). By chance alone there should thus be 6.6 coefficients significant at the .20 level, 3.3 at the .10 level, 1.6 at the .05 level, and 0.3 at the .01 level. The number of significant coefficients for the ethnography characteristics is about twice that expected at each level, suggesting that at least some of these coefficients indicate relationships resulting from something other than chance.

The only ethnography characteristic significant at the .01 level is for "time in the field," which is associated with less positive management relations. Length of time in the field is also associated with lower levels of reported citizenship behaviors. These relationships may result from the substantial length of time required to get sufficiently behind the scenes to observe conflict between workers and management. The importance of this aspect of the ethnographies is consistent with the emphasis that ethnographers place on time spent in the field (Ember & Levinson, 1991).

The following episode, which takes place in an automobile assembly factory, provides an example of conflict between a union shop steward and a supervisor, as reported by an ethnographer who spent a longer than average time in field observation. The history of the episode dates back several years and involves various "unwritten agreements" between the supervisor and the shop steward that the supervisor subsequently violated under pressure from management:

> [Jack Jones, the shop steward] filled in a procedure report calling the supervisor a "perpetual liar." . . . The supervisor went to law, but he wasn't allowed to push it too far. Higher management persuaded him that the case was better dropped and Jack Jones escaped his chance to testify in the dock. (Beynon, 1975, p. 144)

This example suggests that many ongoing conflicts are manifest only in sporadic episodes. Observers spending only a limited amount of time in a setting would be unlikely to observe or to fully understand such conflicts.

The only other ethnography characteristics significant at the .05 level or above involve location: British and European ethnographers report less pride in work (and less organizational citizenship) than U.S. ethnographers. An example of low pride in work appears in an ethnography of a French automobile factory:

Everyone carries out his order as slowly as possible and toward midday the spectacle to these shadows wandering in silence along the dark racks, apparently prey to an incurable lethargy, has something of unreality about it. (Linhart, 1981, p. 108)

These location effects could result either from British and European workers exhibiting less pride and citizenship at given levels of organizational characteristics or from British and European ethnographers reporting lower levels of pride and citizenship at given levels of organizational characteristics. Other data would be necessary to address the difference between these two interpretations. Comparative survey data on U.S., U.K., and European workers, for example, might help adjudicate between these two interpretations.

Observers and participant observers are less likely to report pride in work, and participant observers are less likely to report citizenship behaviors than are ethnographers in the miscellaneous category, which is composed mainly of longtime workers and owners. The intimate workplace knowledge of longtime workers and owners may be necessary to recognize pride in work or organizational citizenship when it is observed. Note, however, that the effects of ethnographers' roles are quite small. The coefficients are significant only at the .20 level and should not be overinterpreted.

The theoretical orientations of the ethnographers produce three methods effects, although none is significant at the .05 level. Functionalists see more pride and citizenship, which is consistent with their positive theoretical orientation about social structures. Feminists also report more citizenship behaviors. Human relations theorists and Marxists evidence no theoretical predispositions across the three aspects of work investigated. The absence of any effects for the year variable suggests that there are no secular trends for any of the three dependent variables.

Turning to the coding process characteristics, there are 45 possible significant coefficients (15 for each dependent variable). By chance alone, there should be 9 coefficients significant at the .20 level, 4.5 at the .10 level, 2.2 at the .05 level, and 0.4 at the .01 level. The number of significant coefficients for the coding process characteristics is about equal to the expected number at each level, suggesting that any observed relationships may result solely from chance.

Acknowledging that any interpretations of coding process effects must by undertaken cautiously, let us see if any interpretable patterns exist. Only one coder effect is significant at the .05 level. Coder 1 reported less positive relations with management than the principal investigator (the omitted category). This effect could result either from selectivity in the books chosen by Coder 1 or from bias. A passage that Coder 1 interpreted as indicating frequent conflict with management (Level 4 of 5) reads as follows:

> There was no suggestion from the women in John's department that management had either the right or the ability to manage. Instead, the women were constantly critical of management. They asked, "When are they going to manage? After all, it's what they get paid for and it's a darn sight more than we get." [Lead workers], especially, were very critical of management:
>
> Jessie Either we've got no work or there's a bloody panic on here. I ask you, what do management do with their time? I reckon I could do better myself than this lot. This place never runs smoothly.
> Vi . . . Management don't know what they're doing.
> Edna I agree, they tell you one thing, you get ready to do it and then it doesn't arrive. We could do better ourselves, I don't know what this lot get paid for. (Westwood, 1982, pp. 25-26)

An obvious bias toward exaggerating conflict is not apparent in the coding of this passage (or in other passages recorded by this coder). Selectivity by this coder in choosing which cases to code remains a possible explanation.

The only coefficient significant at the .01 level for the coding process variables is a contrast between Debriefer 2 and the principal investigator. This debriefer reported more pride in work than the principal investigator. Joint debriefings also resulted in codings of greater pride (significant at the .10 level). Coders met with whichever debriefer was available when they finished a book, thus limiting the likelihood of selectivity and suggesting bias as an explanation. The other coders and the project staff all thought of Debriefer 2 as an especially supportive and affirming person. It is quite possible that Debriefer 2 was more attuned to positive aspects of the ethnographic accounts than the other debriefers and may have influenced coders in that direction during debriefings.

The date on which the ethnography was coded during the coding project has a positive effect on relations with management, but this effect could represent selectivity in the process of choosing which books to code first and which to code later. In addition, the fact that it is one of only three effects significant at the .05 level among 45 possible effects suggests chance as a possible explanation.

In summary, the methods effects associated with the ethnographies and with the coding process add minimally to explained variance, and in no case are their contributions significant at the .05 level. Nevertheless, certain patterns emerge that suggest the possibility of at least some bias in the data.

Patterns of possible bias result mainly from the documentary accounts themselves rather than from the coding process. About twice the number of significant coefficients are observed for the ethnography characteristics as would be expected by chance alone. All the location coefficients indicate more negative work-related experiences and behaviors in European and British accounts than in those from the United States.

Ethnographers' roles also appear to influence the propensity to observe certain behaviors. Most of the coefficients indicate less positive observations about the workplace by observers and participant observers than by the miscellaneous category composed mainly of longtime workers and owners. Amount of time spent in the field by the ethnographers tends to increase the level of negative behaviors and experiences reported.

Theoretical orientations appear to be only modestly related to observers' accounts. Although caution should be exercised in interpreting these coefficients, certain patterns do emerge. Ethnographers appear to observe what their theoretical orientations tell them is important. Thus, functionalists observe pride and citizenship, human relations ethnographers observe solidarity and peer training, and feminists observe citizenship and peer training in the mainly female workforces that are their focus.

For the coding process variables, fewer significant coefficients are observed. The aspect of the coding process with the greatest potential for generating bias appears to be the role of the debriefer. The influence of debriefers ranges across many cases, and slight differences in the checking and debriefing criteria used by debriefers can result in subtle patterns of bias. For these staff members, even more than for coders, continuing training and supervision are especially important.

Additional Reliability and Bias Checks

The reliability and validity of data from documentary accounts can be further analyzed using additional techniques and measures. Many of these techniques are direct applications of widely used techniques for evaluating data quality (Mosteller & Tukey, 1977). The most appropriate measures will vary from project to project.

The effect of missing data on the analysis can be investigated by replacing the missing data with some value, such as the variable mean, and including a dummy variable to designate that the value was imputed for these cases. The effect of this dummy variable will reveal any differences between the cases with real data and imputed data.

Population distributions also can be used to weight the documentary accounts. If the documentary accounts oversample parts of the population, this can be corrected through the use of such weights. The analysis of the weighted data will more accurately reflect the processes as they occur throughout the population of interest. For example, a set of community studies could be weighted to reflect the actual distribution of communities by population size.

A special concern of social scientists has been the possibility of *spatial autocorrelation* between cases. Spatial autocorrelation exists when a case's value on a variable results in part from spatial proximity to other cases exhibiting the phenomenon rather than from underlying causes. Spatial autocorrelation results from a phenomenon diffusing between an area and adjacent areas. Its "cause" in the new area will then be the proximity of the area to the original source of the phenomenon. Such autocorrelation can cloud real causal relationships because the new area acquiring the phenomenon may not possess the underlying causes that normally give rise to it. Autocorrelation can potentially obscure the causes of the development of different technologies or social forms because social forms may spread by diffusion as well as arise from underlying causal factors. Autocorrelation can be modeled and controlled by including a variable that measures proximity between areas (Land & Deane, 1992).

Autocorrelation has wide-ranging implications, and its analysis may be of interest across a variety of topics. For instance, gang violence might exist in an area because of diffusion or contagion rather than because of underlying causes. Controlling for autocorrelation would be important for correctly identifying the underlying causes of gang violence. In addition, the identification of diffusion as a significant cause of the phenomenon could be an important finding in its own right.

In the case of gang violence and other event-related data, temporal autocorrelation also might be of interest as well as spatial autocorrelation. Temporal autocorrelation occurs when the causes of a current phenomenon include s prior level as well as factors operating in the current situation. Both spatial and temporal autocorrelation are significant factors in the determination of many social phenomena and should be explicitly modeled by researchers whenever possible.

Evaluating Validity

Suppose that the measures coded from a set of documentary accounts are coded reliably. Furthermore, no bias in the data is evidenced based on the characteristics of the coders or the primary observers. We still do not know if the variables really indicate what they are intended to indicate. In other words, are they valid indicators of the concepts they are intended to measure?

Validity can be established across four cumulative aspects: face validity, content validity, criterion validity, and construct validity. We will discuss each of these in turn.

Face validity is established by the appearance of validity. For example, suppose we are able to code from documentary accounts the average hours per week that teenagers spend on schoolwork. On face value, this variable is a good measure of how studious the teenagers are. It appears to have good face validity. Face validity is required for establishing validity, but it is not sufficient. We would like to have further indications that time spent on homework effectively measures studiousness.

Content validity is the extent to which a set of indicators measures all the relevant facets or domains of a concept. For instance, studiousness might be conceptualized in the literature as involving paying attention in class, using free time in school for study, number of hours spent on homework per week, and involvement in intellectually oriented hobbies or activities, such as science club or chess club. A good measure of studiousness would include indicators from each of these domains. One of the strengths of documentary accounts is their potential to yield sets of indicators with strong content validity based on the in-depth nature of the information provided.

Criterion validity is established by comparing a measure to some known standard or criterion. The two measures should show the same pattern. For instance, does a measure of self-reported health status correlate positively with medical records for respondents? Good external criterion measures may be difficult to acquire for the cases reported in documentary accounts. However, internal criteria also can be used. Consider job satisfaction. Do organizations with high levels of job satisfaction also have high levels of worker commitment? If they do, this constitutes evidence of criterion validity for the measure of job satisfaction. Divergent validity can also be useful. Do highly satisfied workers exhibit high levels of conflict with managers and with coworkers? If they do, this would be contrary to expectations and should lead to questions about the validity of the measure of job satisfaction being used.

The search for good criterion measures to validate new measures often leads to the examination of related but somewhat distinct concepts, as in the example of job satisfaction and conflict. A concept can be further validated by demonstrating that its relationships with its causes and consequences are as theoretically expected. Such demonstrations show that the concept has construct validity. In other words, as an indicator of a social science construct that is embedded in an accepted theory, the measure is related to its causes and consequences in the manner expected. If it is related in the expected manner, we have increased confidence that it is a good indicator of the underlying concept it is intended to measure. Construct validity builds on the other three forms of validity and is considered essential for full acceptance of a measure as a valid indicator of its intended concept.

Construct validity is thus established by demonstrating consistency between the relationships observed for a new measure and those theoretically expected. The findings on a topic based on the systematic analysis of a set of documentary accounts should thus be consistent with findings based on other types of data, such as surveys and official records. Often, however, findings are somewhat inconsistent across different data sources and methods. These inconsistencies are a potentially rich source of insight and can spur new questions about a research topic.

Construct Validity and Theory Development

The establishment of construct validity is an iterative process involving the interaction among concepts, theories, and data. The introduction of new types of data into the stream of information about a construct can be an especially fruitful moment in the research process. As a relatively new method and one based on a rich data source, the analysis of documentary accounts has the potential to offer new insights on a wide range of constructs and theoretical models in the social sciences.

The process of establishing convergences and divergences between findings based on different types of data is an important impetus to new research and to the development of new theories. Researchers often have noted that documentary accounts sometimes produce different answers to important questions than surveys or government data. For instance, Zetka and Walsh (1994) note that ethnographic accounts generally indicate de-skilling following the introduction of new technology, whereas government data and surveys indicate overall stability or upgrading of skills in the labor force. Zetka and Walsh argue for a more systematic use of ethnographic accounts to generalize findings upward from individual case studies as a strategy for resolving this seeming anomaly. Similarly, Perrucci and Stohl (1997) observe that survey-based analyses of Japanese transplants generally indicate high levels of worker commitment, but observational accounts report speedups, high injury rates, and resentment among workers.

The rapid growth of ethnographies and the inconsistencies being generated between this body of research and survey-based research suggest that we need to explore the information and insights provided by ethnographies more systematically (Eisenhardt, 1989; Pratt & Rafaeli, 1997). Analysis of the large body of ethnographic evidence available across a range of topics has much to offer the social sciences. The systematic analysis of this body of data using techniques that allow the comparison of findings with those derived from other research techniques can be a major boon to theoretical developments in a field. Levinson and Malone (1980, pp. 295-298), for instance, argue that analysis of the HRAF has made significant contributions to the development of anthropological knowledge in the fields of cultural evolution, kinship, expressive culture, socialization, deviance, social problems, and social control.

Analysis of the documentary record also allows the investigation of new variables and relationships that have not previously been explored or that have been slighted in survey research or in research based on social, political, or economic indicators. For instance, one of the most consistent determinants of workers' behaviors, as revealed by the analysis of ethnographic accounts, is working in a well-run organization (Hodson, 1998; see also Hodson, in press). This finding highlights the significant role of organizational effectiveness—a role that has been underanalyzed in survey-based research. Similarly, analysis of the ethnographic record invites fuller investigation of subtle forms of workplace behavior, such as resistance, solidarity, and pride in work, as well as various aspects of informal organizational culture (Trice & Beyer, 1992). Because the ethnographic record includes observations across a significant span of time, analysis of this record can also help establish secular trends or the lack of such trends. These trend lines might otherwise be quite difficult to observe.

Analysis of the documentary record also can suggest new hypotheses that spur the development of new research initiatives using surveys or other methods. For instance, autonomy has been widely identified as an important determinant of positive experiences of work. Analysis of the ethnographic data, however, shows that autonomy is important mainly for work-related outcomes, such as pride, citizenship, and relations with management (Hodson, 1998). Autonomy appears to be less important for coworker-related aspects of worklife, such as solidarity, peer training, and relations with coworkers. Researchers had not previously observed or considered these differential effects of autonomy across different domains of worklife.

Indeed, the entire topic of coworker relations is an area that workplace surveys have slighted. It is impossible to read the ethnographic record on organizations, however, without being impressed by the importance of coworker relations. The importance of coworker relations has been noted since the very beginnings of the industrial relations field, particularly among observers using ethnographic methods (see Homans, 1950). However, the previous noncomparability of findings between ethnographic data and survey data has contributed to only limited attention being paid to coworker relations in survey-based research. The reintroduction of coworker relations to a more central place in the study of industrial relations could be one of many benefits derived from the systematic analysis of documentary accounts. Studies of normative behavior, negotiated orders, and social change in organizations have been identified as additional areas in which documentary accounts have great potential to inform current theories of the workplace (Morrill & Fine, 1997).

6. SUMMARY

This chapter summarizes the gains attainable through the systematic analysis of documentary accounts. The chapter also highlights the key ingredients for successful implementation. Strengths of the method are summarized. The central limitations of the quantitative analysis of documentary accounts—limited population sizes and problems of representativeness—are also highlighted. Finally, we summarize the contributions of document analysis to advancing knowledge in the social sciences.

Why Analyze Documents?

The central contribution of the method is that it transforms rich bodies of descriptive accounts into data sets amenable to quantitative analysis.

Through systematic analysis, researchers can control the effects of confounding factors, identify mediating variables, and establish patterns of causality. Within this framework, the selective use of quoted material to illustrate concepts and relationships can reintroduce the richness of observation found in the original data.

The flexibility of the method is also a strength. Projects can be customized for the study of subtopics within the broader research area. For example, subsets of organizational ethnographies can be further analyzed toward the goal of investigating coworker relations at work.

The content analysis of documentary accounts and the statistical analysis of the resulting data combine the respective strengths of qualitative and quantitative methods. The depth of observation found in documentary accounts allows us to get inside local cultures and situations to observe their hidden life and meanings. The systematic elimination of extraneous, circumstantial covariates through statistical controls and the use of explicit comparison groups allow theories to be tested, unsupported ideas to be rejected, and good ideas to be substantiated.

The systematic analysis of documentary accounts has the ability to make significant contributions to the theoretical development of a variety of fields in the social sciences. An underlying strength of the analysis of documentary accounts of local cultures and situations is that in-depth observations of informal processes can be analyzed across a variety of structural situations. These comparisons allow an analytic bridge to be built between the analysis of microlevel and macrolevel processes.

For example, the study of the ethnographic record on organizations allows important linkages to be made between macrolevel and microlevel theories of the workplace. Today, we live the greater part of our lives within complex organizations. By focusing on the level of the organization and on the even more illusive level of the work group, organizational ethnographies provide us with in-depth access to some of the most central aspects of life in modern society. By systematically analyzing these observations across settings, we can understand these local organizational cultures within the dynamics of the larger political economy (Schwartzman, 1993, p. 66). Conversely, we can understand some of our most personal experiences better by understanding their broader organizational context (Mills, 1959). For social scientists attempting to understand social life in modern societies, studies of informal relations inside formal organizations are of central importance.

Collecting high-quality primary data requires the expenditure of large amounts of time and resources. This is as true in history, political science, and sociology as it is in psychology, medicine, or physics. It is therefore important to make the most effective use of data after they have been collected. In the social sciences, the goal of making effective use of survey data has been advanced by the Inter-University Consortium for Political and Social Research, which today makes thousands of survey-based data sets available to researchers through its member universities. Similarly, the content analysis of bodies of documentary observation has a potentially significant role in making more efficient use of existing qualitative data. Without the systematic analysis of bodies of documentary evidence, however, the richness of documentary accounts will be used mainly for texture and for generating hypotheses to be tested using other techniques. Extant bodies of documentary evidence have much more to offer than this. Because documentary accounts are based on in-depth observation, they have the potential to expand our conceptual and theoretical toolkits in important new directions.

Guidelines for Implementation

After specifying the theoretical question to be addressed, the researcher must next identify a suitable population of documentary accounts. Detailed coding strategies and protocols must be developed to increase reliability and validity. Finally, advanced planning is needed to allow the measurement of reliability after the coding is completed. Three sets of tasks thus frame the process of initiating an analysis of documentary accounts: (a) defining the population of cases and selecting the cases systematically, (b) developing a comprehensive and reliable coding instrument, and (c) building in checks for reliability and bias.

The cases to be analyzed should be selected in such a way that the full population of available cases is identified and considered. As the first step in this process, the researcher must carefully define the population of documentary accounts of theoretical interest. Defining the population of interest requires that the researcher be knowledgeable not only about the types of accounts that fall within the selection criteria but also about related types of documents that fall outside the criteria of inclusion. If the population of documents is too large to include all cases, then it can be further restricted on theoretically relevant dimensions. For instance, the population can be restricted to the cases from the most recent decade or by narrowing the focus of the study. Alternatively, a random sample of cases can be selected for analysis if the researcher wants to include the full time span and a wide definition of the topic.

If the population of available cases is too small, it can be widened by including articles, dissertations, or unpublished conference papers in addition to book-length accounts. These additions are also useful if the researcher wants to expand the project at a later time.

Coding instruments should be comprehensive of the topics of interest and should provide complete information on key concepts. The length of the coding instrument is not constrained by respondent cooperation as in the case of surveys; documentary accounts treated as respondents can be interrogated for as long as the coder wants. The instrument can easily include 100 to 200 variables. Given the available length, researchers have the opportunity to code a wide range of variables for later analysis. Too lengthy an instrument, however, may decrease reliability if coders are unable to keep in mind all the variables that need to be coded.

Reliability needs to be built into the coding process by the use of questions that have concrete referents in the accounts. Researchers should disaggregate abstract concepts into simpler factual questions that do not require excessive inference. Detailed protocols for coding questions need to be developed before the main coding operation begins and need to be updated as coding proceeds. Coding a 10% sample of cases with multiple coders will allow important reliability checks to be undertaken during the analysis stage (Elder et al., 1993). Detailed information on the coders and, especially, on the documentary accounts and their underlying methods and assumptions need to be recorded. This information will allow additional reliability and bias checks in the analysis stage. These methods-oriented analyses can provide extremely valuable information that is useful for the development of both quantitative and qualitative methods as applied to the research area being studied. They are an important supplement to the analysis of the substantive topics under consideration.

Strengths

The fundamental contribution of the systematic analysis of documentary accounts is that it creates an analytic link between the in-depth accounts of professional observers and the statistical methods of quantitative researchers. This link can then be used to test hypotheses generated from qualitative research as well as hypotheses derived from quantitative research methods. The conclusions derived from these analyses are potentially generalizable and are open to debate, cross-examination, and cross-validation.

The systematic analysis of documentary accounts thus combines the strengths of qualitative and quantitative approaches. The method combines detailed measurement based on in-depth observation with the analytic power of quantitative analysis (Zetka & Walsh, 1994, p. 43). The measures used have potentially high validity, and the concepts have potentially great relevance to the issues being studied. Problems associated with the sometimes limited validity and relevance of survey data and government statistics can thus be directly addressed by this method. The method may also spur the development of new concepts and measures with greater relevance that can later be included in survey instruments.

The method adds the rigor of hypothesis testing, explicit comparison groups, and controls to qualitative analyses. As Walton (1992) argues, case studies "drift without anchor unless they are incorporated into some typology of general processes, made causally explicit within the case, and ultimately referred back to the universe which the case represents" (p. 124). Evaluation of a broader range of cases increases the variation available for analysis. Because the researcher evaluates a large number of cases, irrelevant variables will be likely to vary randomly rather than becoming a focus of analysis and interpretation because of chance concurrence with the phenomenon of interest (Levinson & Malone, 1980). Analyzing a large set of cases also allows the introduction of variation at higher levels of analysis, such as the organizational level for workplace studies or the school or community level for studies of educational outcomes. Many of the important causes of educational outcomes, for example, may be operating at these higher levels of analysis. Without variation across these levels, individual case studies cannot uncover the important causes of the phenomena that they are studying.

The analysis of sets of documentary accounts also encourages greater objectivity in the analysis of these accounts. Theory testing is spatially and temporally separated from the primary data collection. This reduces the possibility of intentionally or unintentionally skewing the data in favor of the theory being tested. In addition, explicit tests of bias in coding the data can be introduced—tests that are impossible when considering only one case at a time.

Systematic analysis of documentary accounts can thus provide tentative answers to some of the questions currently proposed by constructivist critiques of social science knowledge. The biases embodied in documentary accounts can be conceptualized, measured, evaluated, and discussed.

The systematic quantitative analysis of documentary accounts can thus provide a truly radical "source analysis" of the various subjectivities used by professionals in producing detailed observational records (Tobin, 1990). The systematic analysis of documentary accounts has the potential to achieve the sort of intersubjectivity that is considered a worthy but largely unobtainable goal by constructivists (Denzin & Lincoln, 1994). The goal of establishing intersubjectivity is unobtainable when each account is analyzed separately. When systematically analyzing sets of accounts, however, subjectivities can be identified, and intersubjectivity becomes a realizable goal.

Perhaps the most important advantage of systematic studies of documentary accounts, as opposed to their analysis as isolated case studies, is an increased ability to reject outdated ideas. A major challenge for science is to recognize and reject "well meaning but incorrect theories that pass for knowledge" (Ember & Levinson, 1991, p. 79). "Just as mutations arise naturally but not all are beneficial, so [theories] emerge naturally but not all are correct. If progress is to occur, therefore, we require a . . . mechanism of selection" (Caws, 1969, p. 1378). The tools of systematic quantitative analysis provide a mechanism by which ideas that are unsupported can be identified and discredited. Analyses based on single cases are limited in their ability to provide convincing evidence that a hypothesized theoretical connection is not working. Other cases may exist in which it does operate. The analysis of multiple cases opens the door to the important work of sorting between theories of causality based on strong supporting evidence, on one hand, and theoretical propositions based on nongeneralizable events, on the other.

An additional important benefit of the systematic analysis of documentary accounts is their ability to spur advances in *construct development*. For instance, a striking finding derived from the analysis of organizational ethnographies is the widespread negative effect of management incompetence and organizational ineffectiveness on individuals' experiences of work (Hodson, 1998). Survey-based analyses have not highlighted this aspect of organizational life, perhaps in part because of difficulties in measuring management incompetence and organizational effectiveness using survey methods. Ethnographers, in contrast, generally give detailed reports on these aspects of organizational life. Given the apparent importance of organizational effectiveness, survey-based research investigations of the workplace might consider attempting to develop new measures of this important dimension of organizational life.

Flexibility for addressing a range of topics and subtopics is another strength of the systematic analysis of documentary accounts. Descriptive accounts are generally rich, not just in depth but also in the range of topics covered. Indeed, one standard measure of a good documentary account is the provision of reasonably comprehensive descriptions of the context that situates a specific situation or event. The range of the topics covered creates the opportunity for data sets to include a wide range of topics, thus greatly increasing their value as data archives.

Finally, the systematic analysis of documentary accounts is cumulative and allows later additions and extensions over time. The continuing expansion of the Human Relations Area Files provides a case in point (Ember & Levinson, 1991). Diverse researchers can use the archives and can contribute to and expand them over time. Because documents accumulate across time, the opportunity to study time trends also becomes a possibility. (For a similar argument about the benefits of analyzing archived survey data, see Kiecolt & Nathan, 1985, p. 11.) The cumulative aspect of the coding of documentary accounts greatly increases the utility of what is already a cost-effective method.

Limitations

The systematic analysis of documentary records faces certain challenges and limitations concerning both the nature of the data and the available cases to be analyzed. Categorization, coding, and quantification result in the loss of some of the richness of the original observations (Levinson & Malone, 1980, p. 9). The data used will be less sensitive and less precise than the data presented in individual case studies. This sacrifice in the depth and validity of indicators occurs as part of a trade-off to achieve increased generalizability and the ability to sort between defensible and less defensible conclusions.

The secondary user of documentary accounts has no control over the topics covered or omitted. Missing data will be substantial for some topics. Data imputation and proxies will have to be used in some situations. Sensitivity analysis and subsample analysis may also provide partial solutions.

The set of cases to be studied will inevitably be a conglomerate of convenience samples, each with an N of 1. Inferential statistics are inappropriate for generalizing from this population to the broader population of all cases of the phenomenon of interest. Generalizations from the analysis therefore must be made with caution. Such generalizations must be defended with evidence about the relationship between the set of cases and the broader population of interest. Because the set of cases is not generally a random sample of the population of interest, tests of significance are not sufficient for establishing this relationship.

For some topics, the available set of cases may be too small and diverse to analyze. If the set of available studies for a particular research topic is too small, a systematic analysis of these cases may not be fruitful. (For a similar discussion of the effects of population size and diversity on quantitative meta-analysis, see Wolf, 1986.)

Even if the population of available cases is large, estimates of population parameters based on the analysis of documentary accounts are generally not appropriate. Such estimates should be made only from large representative samples such as census data or major national surveys. As with all methods, the systematic analysis of documentary accounts is best used as part of an ongoing research dialogue involving contributions from a variety of methods.

Contributions to Social Science Knowledge

The content analysis of documentary accounts is a rapidly growing method in the social sciences. New knowledge derived from this method will have an increasing influence on social science theories in coming years. The methods discussed in this monograph suggest the possibility of achieving theoretical advances from the systematic analysis of such accounts through establishing areas of cross-methods convergence and divergence. In addition, new concepts and relationships can be explored and new research questions generated.

It is hoped that the ideas presented in this monograph will be of assistance to researchers as they attempt to make use of the wealth of documentary accounts to advance social science knowledge. Textual documents, including documentary accounts, are increasingly common sources of information for the social sciences. The widespread availability of electronic scanning technology, the increased accessibility of online archives, and the potential for advanced autocoding technologies further increase the accessibility of these documents as data sources. The systematic analysis of these documents through the application of standard scientific techniques of population definition, sampling, systematic coding, and statistical analysis can lead to rapid gains in knowledge about the topics studied.

A New Window on the Social World

The social sciences have traditionally relied on four principal sources of data: surveys, government statistics, field observation, and experiments (Singleton, Straits, & Straits, 1993). Surveys are the most widely used method of gathering information, and experiments are the least widely used. In recent years, the content analysis of textual documents has become a fifth major method of acquiring data useful to the social science enterprise. An examination of the data used in articles published in leading social science journals suggests that analysis of documentary data already has eclipsed experiments and rivals field observation and government statistics in prevalence, range, and utility.

The systematic analysis of material that has previously been used only in a case study format provides exciting new opportunities for social scientists. The analysis of these new data sources can provide a basis for important new findings and conceptual breakthroughs across a variety of fields of study in the social sciences.

APPENDIX

WORKPLACE ETHNOGRAPHY CODE SHEET

CASEID: _____

DATE: **q1**(Mo=) **q1a**(Da=) **q1b**(Yr=)
CODER: **q2** (2 col):   BOOK CODE: **q3** (3 col):

T1   BOOK TITLE AND AUTHOR'S LAST NAME: _____

_____

T2   MODAL OCCUPATION: _____   Page #s: (Include in Text)

T3   INDUSTRY: _____   Page #s: (Include in Text)

T4   COUNTRY/REGION: _____   Page #s: (Include in Text)

T5   OBSERVER'S ROLE: _____   Page #s: (Include in Text)

of1   YEAR STUDY BEGAN: _____   9999 - No Info   Page #s

of1a   YEAR STUDY ENDED: _____   9999 - No Info   Page #s:

74

ORGANIZATIONAL FACTORS

Technology/organization

of2a Occupation: 00 - Professional 01 - Management/Supervisor 02 - Clerical 03 - Sales 04 - Skilled 05 - Assembly 06 - Unskilled 07 - Service 08 - Farm 09 - No Info Page #s:

of2b Craft: 1 - Yes 2 - No 9 - No Info Page #s:

of2c Direct Supervision: 1 - Yes 2 - No 9 - No Info Page #s:

of2d Bench: 1 - Straight Piece 2 - Quota/Bonus 3 - Hourly Guaranteed 4 - No Bench 9 - No Info Page #s:

of2e Assembly Line: 1 - Yes 2 - No 9 - No Info Page #s:

of2f Automated: 1 - Yes 2 - No 9 - No Info Page #s:

of2g Microchip: 1 - Yes 2 - No 9 - No Info Page #s:

of2h Bureaucratic: 1 - Yes 2 - No 9 - No Info Page #s:

of2i Corporatist: 1 - Yes 2 - No 9 - No Info Page #s:

of2j Worker Ownership: 1 - Co-op 2 - ESOP 3 - None 9 - No Info Page #s:

of3 Employment Size: (6 col): _____ 999999 - No Info Page #s:

of4 Employment Growth: 1 - Decline 2 - Stable 3 - Growing 9 - No Info Page #s:

of5 Level of Competition: 1 - Low 2 - Medium 3 - High 9 - No Info Page #s:

of6 Product Market Stability: 1 - Stable 2 - Unstable 9 - No Info Page #s:

of7 Productivity: 1 - Declining 2 - Stable 3 - Increasing 9 - No Info Page #s:

of8 Locally Owned: 1 - Yes 2 - No 9 - No Info Page #s:

of9 Subcontractor: 1 - Yes 2 - No 9 - No Info Page #s:

of10 Divisional Status: 1 - Yes 2 - No 9 - No Info Page #s:

of11 Owned by a Conglomerate: 1 - Yes 2 - No 9 - No Info Page #s:

of12 Corporate Headquarters: 1 - Yes 2 - No 9 - No Info Page #s:

of13 Corporate Sector: 1 - Core 2 - Periphery 3 - Industrial 4 - Combined 9 - No Info Page #s:

of14 Unions (type): 1 - None 2 - Craft 3 - Industrial 4 - Combined 9 - No Info Page #s:

of15 Unions (strength): 1 - Weak 2 - Average 3 - Strong 7 - NA 9 - No Info Page #s:

of16 Turnover: 1 - Low 2 - Medium 3 - High 9 - No Info Page #s:

of17 Layoff Frequency: 1 - Never 2 - Seldom 3 - Sometimes 4 - Frequent 9 - No Info Page #s:

(continued)

APPENDIX Continued

of18	Grievance Procedure:	1 - Union Run	2 - Company Run	3 - None	9 - No Info	Page #s:
of19	Ilm (range):	1 - No Workers	2 - Few	3 - Some	4 - Many	5 - Most	6 - All	9 - No Info	Page #s:
of20	Ilm (steps):	(2 col, 00 - 07)	08 - Eight or more	99 - No Info	Page #s:
of21	Sexual Division of Labor:	1 - Yes	2 - Integrated	9 - No Info	Page #s:
of22	Racial Division of Labor:	1 - Yes	2 - Integrated	9 - No Info	Page #s:
of23	Quality Control:	1 - Govt Inspector	2 - QC Inspector	3 - Supervisor	4 - Self	9 - No Info	Page #s:
of24	Solicitation of Worker Involvement:	1 - Never Asked	2 - Informal	3 - Formal	9 - No Info	Page #s:
of25	QWL Program:	1 - Yes	2 - No	9 - No Info	Page #s:
of26	Union-Management Partnership:	1 - Yes	2 - No	9 - No Info	Page #s:
of27	Organizational Communications:	1 - Poor	2 - Average	3 - Good	9 - No Info	Page #s:
of28	Organization Reproduction (recruitment):	1 - Little effort	2 - Average effort	3 - Great effort	9 - No Info	Page #s:
of29	Level of Repair:	1 - Poor	2 - Average	3 - Good	9 - No Info	Page #s:

Labor Force Composition

o30a Gender (% female): _____ (3 col)   999 - No Info   Page #s:
o30b Race (% minority): _____ (3 col)   999 - No Info   Page #s:

T6 Name of Ethnic Group: _____   Page #s: (Include in Text)

o30c Age (median): _____ (2 col)   99 - No Info   Page #s:
o30d Seniority (median): _____ (2 col)   99 - No Info   Page #s: (LE 6 months = 00; approximately 1 year = 01)

MANAGEMENT

mt1	Leadership:	1 - Catastrophic	2 - Marginal	3 - Adequate	4 - Good	5 - Exceptional	9 - No Info	Page #:
mt2	Organization of Production:	1 - Catastrophic	2 - Marginal	3 - Adequate	4 - Good	5 - Exceptional	9 - No Info	Page #:
mt3	Abusive:	1 - Never	2 - Rarely	3 - Sometimes	4 - Frequently	5 - Constantly	9 - No Info	Page #:
mt4	Paternalistic:	1 - Yes	2 - No	9 - No Info	Page #s:
mt5	Sexual Harassment:	1 - None	2 - Condescending	3 - Jokes	4 - Overly Personal	5 - Touch	6 - Threats/Promises	7 - Forced Sexual Contact	9 - No Info	Page #s:

Control Strategies

mt6a	Increase Inspections:	1 - Yes	2 - No	9 - No Info	Page #s:
mt6b	Reorganize Tasks:	1 - Yes	2 - No	9 - No Info	Page #s:
mt6c	Change Technology:	1 - Yes	2 - No	9 - No Info	Page #s:
mt6d	Restrict Pay:	1 - Yes	2 - No	9 - No Info	Page #s:
mt6e	Restrict Hours:	1 - Yes	2 - No	9 - No Info	Page #s:
mt6f	Demotions:	1 - Yes	2 - No	9 - No Info	Page #s:
mt6g	Firings:	1 - Yes	2 - No	9 - No Info	Page #s:

COMMUNITY FACTORS

cf1	Unemployment:	1 - Low	2 - Medium	3 - High	9 - No Info	Page #s:	
cf2	Rural/Urban:	1 - Rural	2 - Small Town	3 - Medium Town	4 - City	9 - No Info	Page #s:

WORKERS

w1	Job Satisfaction:	1 - Very Low	2 - Moderately Low	3 - Average	4 - High	5 - Very High	9 - No Info Page #s:
w2	Pay:	1 - Very Low	2 - Moderately Low	3 - Average	4 - High	5 - Very High	9 - No Info Page #s:
w3	Benefit Package:	1 - None	2 - Minimal	3 - Average	4 - High	9 - No Info	Page #s:
w4	Job Security:	1 - None	2 - Minimal	3 - Average	4 - High	9 - No Info	Page #s:
w5	Effort Bargain:	1 - Extra Effort Given Freely					
		2 - Conditional Effort Given					
		3 - Reticence Practiced Widely					
		9 - No Info Page #s:					

Conflict With Management/Supervisors

w6a	Frequency of Conflict With Managers:	1 - Never	2 - Infrequent	3 - Average	4 - Frequent	5 - Constant	9 - No Info Page #s:
w6b	Frequency of Conflict With Supervisors:	1 - Never	2 - Infrequent	3 - Average	4 - Frequent	5 - Constant	9 - No Info Page #s:

(continued)

TRAINING

w7a Job Required Skill: 1 - Speed and Dexterity Only 2 - Some Complexity 3 - Highly Complex 9 - No Info Page #s:

w7b Modal Completed Academic Education: 1 - Grade School 2 - Secondary School 3 - Two-Year Program 4 - Bachelor's Degree 5 - Graduate 9 - No Info Page #s:

w7c Modal Vo-Tech Education: 1 - None 2 - Less Than One Year 3 - More Than One Year 9 - No Info Page #s:

w7d OJT Training: 1 - None 2 - Very Little 3 - Average 4 - More Than Average 5 - Extensive 9 - No Info Page #s:

w7e Informal Peer Training: 1 - None 2 - Very Little 3 - Average 4 - More Than Average 5 - Extensive 9 - No Info Page #s:

w7f Experience/Insider Knowledge Used: 1 - None 2 - Very Little 3 - Average 4 - More Than Average 5 - Extensive 9 - No Info Page #s:

w7g Previously Existing Skills: 1 - Life Experiences 2 - None 9 - No Info Page #s:

WORKER STRATEGIES

w8a Strikes: 1 - None 2 - Informal Nonviolent 3 - Informal Violent 4 - Formal Nonviolent 5 - Formal Violent 9 - No Info Page #s:

w8b Strike Length (in days): (4 col) 9997 - NA 9999 - No Info 9999 - No Info Page #s:

w8c History of Strikes: 1 - No 2 - Infrequent 3 - Frequent 9 - No Info Page #s:

w8d Machine Sabotage: 1 - No 2 - Yes 9 - No Info Page #s:

w8e Procedure Sabotage: 1 - No 2 - Yes 9 - No Info Page #s:

w8f Social Sabotage: 1 - No 2 - Yes 9 - No Info Page #s:

w8g Subvert Particular Manager: 1 - No 2 - Yes 9 - No Info Page #s:

w8h Theft: 1 - No 2 - Yes 9 - No Info Page #s:

w8i Playing Dumb: 1 - No 2 - Yes 9 - No Info Page #s:

w8j Withhold Enthusiasm: 1 - No 2 - Yes 9 - No Info Page #s:

w8k Work Avoidance/Withdrawal: 1 - No 2 - Yes 9 - No Info Page #s:

w8l Absenteeism: 1 - No 2 - Yes 9 - No Info Page #s:

w8m Quits: 1 - No 2 - Yes 9 - No Info Page #s:

w8n Good Soldier: 1 - None 2 - Some 3 - Half 4 - Most 5 - All 9 - No Info Page #s:

w8o Smooth Operator: 1 - None 2 - Some 3 - Half 4 - Most 5 - All 9 - No Info Page #s:

w8p Making Out: 1 - None 2 - Some 3 - Half 4 - Most 5 - All 9 - No Info Page #s:

w8q Brown-Nosing: 1 - None 2 - Some 3 - Half 4 - Most 5 - All 9 - No Info Page #s:

w8r Making Up Games: 1 - Yes 2 - No 9 - No Info Page #s:

w8s Making Up Social Activities: 1 - Yes 2 - No 9 - No Info Page #s:

CONDITIONS OF CONSENT/COMPLIANCE

w9a	Economic Necessity:	1 - Yes	2 - No	9 - No Info		Page #:
w9b	Loyal to Particular Manager:	1 - Yes	2 - No	9 - No Info		Page #:
w9c	Commitment to Organizational Goals:	1 - Yes	2 - No	9 - No Info		Page #:
w9d	Pride in Work:	1 - Rare	2 - Average	3 - A Great Deal	9 - No Info	Page #:
w9e	Social Friendship:	1 - Yes	2 - No	9 - No Info		Page #:

NATURE OF CONSENT/COMPLIANCE

w10a	Extra Effort:	1 - Yes	2 - No	9 - No Info	Page #:
w10b	Extra Time:	1 - Yes	2 - No	9 - No Info	Page #:
w10c	Cooperation:	1 - Absent	2 - Mixed	3 - Widespread	9 - No Info Page #:

NATURE OF WORK

nw1	Autonomy:	1 - None	2 - Little	3 - Average	4 - High	5 - Very High	9 - No Info Page #:
nw2	Creativity:	1 - None	2 - Little	3 - Average	4 - High	5 - Very High	9 - No Info Page #:
nw3	Meaningful Work:	1 - Meaningless	2 - Somewhat Meaningful	3 - Fulfilling	9 - No Info Page #:		
nw4	Freedom of Movement:	1 - Little or None	2 - Average	3 - A Great Deal	9 - No Info Page #:		
nw5	Pace (difficulty):	1 - Easy	2 - Average	3 - Difficult	4 - Brutal	9 - No Info Page #:	
nw6	Pace (variability):	1 - Steady	2 - Irregular	9 - No Info Page #:			
nw7	Physical Demands of Work:	1 - Easy	2 - Average	3 - Difficult	4 - Brutal	9 - No Info Page #:	
nw8	Comfort of Work Area:	1 - Comfortable	2 - Average	3 - Unpleasant	9 - No Info Page #:		
nw9	Injuries:	1 - None or Rare	2 - Average	3 - Common	9 - No Info Page #:		

FOCAL GROUP

fg1	Focal Group:	1 - All Work Individual	2 - Fluid Subgroups	3 - Permanent Subgroups	9 - No Info Page #:		
fg2	Size of Focal Group:	(3 col)	999 - No Info Page #:				
fg3	Focal Group Cohesion:	1 - Absent	2 - Infrequent	3 - Average	4 - Widespread	5 - Pervasive	9 - No Info Page #:
fg4	Leadership (within group):	1 - Absent	2 - Average	3 - Strong	9 - No Info Page #:		
fg5	Solidarity (mutual defense):	1 - Absent	2 - Average	3 - Strong	9 - No Info Page #:		
fg6	Discipline Enforced by Workers:	1 - Never	2 - Occasionally	3 - Frequently	4 - Principally	9 - No Info Page #:	
fg7	Group Boundaries:	1 - Nonexistent	2 - Weak	3 - Average	4 - Strong	5 - Very Strong	9 - No Info Page #:

(continued)

APPENDIX Continued

fg8   Alternative Status Hierarchies: 1 - Nonexistent   2 - Occasional   3 - Clearly Articulated   9 - No Info   Page #s:

fg9   Task Groups Self-Monitoring: 1 - Yes   2 - No   9 - No Info   Page #s:

fg10 Organized Group Conflict
With Management/Supervisors: 1 - Absent   2 - Infrequent   3 - Average   4 - Widespread   5 - Pervasive   9 - No Info   Page #s:

fg11 Within-Group Conflict: 1 - Nonexistent   2 - Occasional   3 - Frequent   9 - No Info   Page #s:

g11a Gossip: 1 - Yes   2 - No   9 - No Info   Page #s:

g11b Interference: 1 - Yes   2 - No   9 - No Info   Page #s:

fg12 Between-Group Conflict: 1 - Nonexistent   2 - Occasional   3 - Frequent   9 - No Info   Page #s:

g12a Gossip: 1 - Yes   2 - No   9 - No Info   Page #s:

g12b Interference: 1 - Yes   2 - No   9 - No Info   Page #s:

fg13 Basis of Alternative Social
Groups at Work: 1 - Age   2 - Gender   3 - Race/Ethnicity   4 - No Alternative Social Grouping   9 - No Info   Page #s:

fg14 Do Work Friendships Carry Over to Outside? 1 - Yes   2 - No   9 - No Info   Page #s:

COMMENTS

REFERENCES

ABBOTT, A. (1992) "From causes to events: Notes on narrative positivism." *Sociological Methods and Research* 20: 428-455.

ABBOTT, A., and HRYCAK, A. (1990) "Measuring resemblance in sequence data." *American Journal of Sociology* 96: 144-185.

ADLER, P. A., and ADLER, P. (1995) "The demography of ethnography." *Journal of Contemporary Ethnography* 24: 3-29.

AMINZADE, R. (1992) "Historical sociology and time." *Sociological Methods and Research* 20: 456-480.

APPLEBAUM, E. R., and BATT, R. (1994) *The New American Workplace.* Ithaca, NY: Industrial and Labor Relations Press.

APPLEBAUM, H. (1981) *Royal Blue: The Culture of Construction Workers.* New York: Holt.

BABB, S. (1996) " 'A true American system of finance': Frame resonance in the U.S. labor movement, 1866 to 1886." *American Sociological Review* 61: 1033-1052.

BARRY, H., III, and SCHLEGEL, A. (eds.). (1980) *Cross-Cultural Samples and Codes.* Pittsburgh, PA: University of Pittsburgh Press.

DAUM, L. (1995) "Measuring policy change in the Rehnquist court." *American Politics Quarterly* 23: 373-382.

BERNARD, H. R. (1988) *Research Methods in Cultural Anthropology.* Newbury Park, CA: Sage.

BERNARD, H. R., and RYAN, G. W. (1998) "Textual analysis: Qualitative and quantitative methods," in H. R. Bernard (ed.), *Handbook of Methods in Cultural Anthropology,* pp. 595-646. Walnut Creek, CA: Altamira.

BEYNON, H. (1975) *Working for Ford.* East Ardsley, UK: E. P. Publishing.

BEYNON, H., and BLACKBURN, R. M. (1972) *Perceptions of Work.* Cambridge, UK: Cambridge University Press.

BIGGART, N. (1989) *Charismatic Capitalism.* Chicago: University of Chicago Press.

BLAUNER, R. (1964) *Alienation and Freedom.* Chicago: University of Chicago Press.

BOND, D., JENKINS, J. C., TAYLOR, C. L., and SCHOCK, K. (1997) "Mapping mass political conflict and civil society: Issues and prospects for the automated development of event data." *Journal of Conflict Resolution* 41: 533-579.

BURAWOY, M. (1979) *Manufacturing Consent.* Chicago: University of Chicago Press.

BURAWOY, M. (1991) "The extended case study method," in M. Burawoy (ed.), *Ethnography Unbound,* pp. 271-290. Berkeley: University of California Press.

BURGESS, R. G. (1995) *Studies in Qualitative Methodology.* Greenwich, CT: JAI.

BURRIS, B. H. (1983) *No Room at the Top.* New York: Praeger.

CASTLES, F., and MAIR, P. (1984) "Left-right political scales: Some expert judgements." *European Journal of Political Research* 12: 73-88.

CAWS, P. (1969, December 12) "The structure of discovery." *Science,* pp. 1375-1380.

CLARK, D. J. (1997) *Like Day and Night: Unionizing in a Southern Mill Town.* Chapel Hill: University of North Carolina Press.

CLAWSON, D., and SU, T. T. (1990) "Was 1980 special? A comparison of 1980 and 1986 corporate PAC contributions." *Sociological Quarterly* 31: 371-387.

COFFIN, F. M. (1994) *On Appeal: Courts, Lawyering and Judging.* New York: Norton.

COHEN, J., and COHEN, P. (1983) *Applied Multiple Regression/Correlation Analysis for the Behavioral Sciences.* Hillsdale, NJ: Lawrence Erlbaum.

COOK, T. (1992) *Meta-Analysis for Explanation.* New York: Russell Sage.

CORNFIELD, D. B., and FLETCHER, B. (1998) "Institutional constraints on social movement 'frame extension.' " *Social Forces* 76: 1305-1321.

CRESS, D. M., and SNOW, D. A. (1996) "Mobilization at the margins." *American Sociological Review* 61: 1089-1109.

CROZIER, M. (1971) *The World of the Office Worker.* Translated by D. Landau. Chicago: University of Chicago Press.

DALTON, M. (1959) *Men Who Manage.* New York: John Wiley.

DAVIS, S. (1989) *Justice Rehnquist and the Constitution.* Princeton, NJ: Princeton University Press.

DEMOS, J. (1970) *A Little Commonwealth: Family Life in Plymouth Colony.* New York: Oxford University Press.

DENZIN, N. K., and LINCOLN, Y. S. (1994) *Handbook of Qualitative Research.* Thousand Oaks, CA: Sage.

DEUTSCHER, I., PESTELLO, F. P., and PESTELLO, H. F. G. (1993) *Sentiments and Acts.* Hawthorne, NY: Aldine.

DOHAN, D. P., and SANCHEZ-JANKOWSKI, M. (1998) "Using computers to analyze ethnographic field data," in J. Hagan and K. S. Cook (eds.), *Annual Review of Sociology,* pp. 477-498. Palo Alto, CA: Annual Reviews.

DOUGLAS, W. O. (1980) *The Court Years, 1939-1975.* New York: Random House.

DUNTEMAN, G. H. (1989) *Principal Components Analysis.* Quantitative Applications in the Social Sciences, 69. Newbury Park, CA: Sage.

EDWARDS, G. C., III, KESSEL, J. H., and ROCKMAN, B. A. (1993) *Researching the Presidency.* Pittsburgh, PA: University of Pittsburgh Press.

EISENHARDT, K. M. (1989) "Building theories from case study research." *Academy of Management Review* 14: 532-550.

ELDER, G. H., PAVALKO, E. K., and CLIPP, E. C. (1993) *Working With Archival Data.* Quantitative Applications in the Social Sciences, 88. Newbury Park, CA: Sage.

EMBER, C. R., and LEVINSON, D. (1991) "The substantive contributions of worldwide cross-cultural studies using secondary data." *Behavior Science Research* 25: 79-140.

FEAGIN, J. R., ORUM, A. M., and SJOBERG, G. (eds.) (1991) *A Case for the Case Study.* Chapel Hill: University of North Carolina Press.

FINLAY, W. (1988) *Work on the Waterfront.* Philadelphia, PA: Temple University Press.

FORMISANO, R. P. (1983) *The Transformation of Political Culture.* New York: Oxford University Press.

FRANZOSI, R. (1990) "Strategies for the prevention, detection, and correction of measurement error in data collected from textual sources." *Sociological Methods and Research* 18: 442-472.

FRANZOSI, R. (1995) *The Puzzle of Strikes.* Cambridge, UK: Cambridge University Press.

FRANZOSI, R. (1998) "Narrative analysis: Or why (and how) sociologists should be interested in narrative," in J. Hagan and K. S. Cook (eds.), *Annual Review of Sociology,* pp. 517-554. Palo Alto, CA: Annual Reviews.

FRANZOSI, R. (1999) *From Words to Numbers: Narrative as Data.* Cambridge, UK: Cambridge University Press.

FREDRICKSON, G. M. (1997) *The Comparative Imagination.* Berkeley: University of California Press.

GAILUS, M. (1994) "Food riots in Germany in the late 1840s." *Past and Present* 145: 157-193.

GAMSON, W. A. (1975) *The Strategy of Social Protest.* Homewood, IL: Dorsey.

GOULDNER, A. W. (1964) *Patterns of Industrial Bureaucracy.* New York: Free Press.

GRAHAM, L. (1995) *On the Line at Subaru-Isuzu.* Ithaca, NY: Industrial and Labor Relations Press.

GREENBERG, E. S. (1986) *Workplace Democracy.* Ithaca, NY: Cornell University Press.

GRENIER, G. J. (1988) *Inhuman Relations.* Philadelphia, PA: Temple University Press.

GRIFFIN, L. J. (1993) "Narratives, event-structure analysis, and causal interpretation in historical sociology." *American Journal of Sociology* 98: 1094-1133.

GRISWOLD, W. (1992) "The writing on the mud wall." *American Sociological Review* 57: 709-724.

GUBA, E. G., and LINCOLN, Y. S. (1994) "Competing paradigms in qualitative research," in N. K. Denzin and Y. S. Lincoln (eds.), *Handbook of Qualitative Research,* pp. 105-117. Thousand Oaks, CA: Sage.

GUNTHER, G. (1994) *Learned Hand: The Man and the Judge.* New York: Knopf.

HAREVEN, T. (1982) *Family Time and Industrial Time.* Cambridge, UK: Cambridge University Press.

HART, P. (1997) "The geography of revolution in Ireland 1917-1923." *Past and Present* 155: 142-176.

HARVARD UNIVERSITY (1998) *Comprehensive Teaching Materials Catalog.* Cambridge, MA: Harvard University Press. Available: www.hbsp.harvard.edu.

HERMANN, M. G., and HAGAN, J. D. (1998) "International decision making." *Foreign Policy* 110: 124-137.

HICKS, A., and KENWORTHY, L. (1998) "Cooperation and political economic performance in affluent democratic capitalism." *American Journal of Sociology* 103: 1631-1672.

HODSON, R. (1995) "Cohesion or conflict? Race, solidarity, and resistance in the workplace," in R. L. Simpson and I. H. Simpson (eds.), *Research in the Sociology of Work: Vol. 5. The Meaning of Work,* pp. 135-159. Greenwich, CT: JAI.

HODSON, R. (1996) "Dignity in the workplace under participative management: *Alienation and Freedom* revisited." *American Sociological Review* 61: 719-738.

HODSON, R. (1998) "Organizational ethnographies: An underutilized resource in the sociology of work." *Social Forces* 76: 1173-1208.

HODSON, R. (In press) *Working With Dignity.* Cambridge, UK: Cambridge University Press.

HODSON, R., WELSH, S., RIEBLE, S., JAMISON, C. S., and CREIGHTON, S. (1993) "Is worker solidarity undermined by autonomy and participation? Patterns from the ethnographic literature." *American Sociological Review* 58: 398-416.

HOMANS, G. C. (1950) *The Human Group.* New York: Harcourt, Brace.

KALTON, G. (1983) *Introduction to Survey Sampling.* Quantitative Applications in the Social Sciences, 35. Beverly Hills, CA: Sage.

KAMATA, S. (1982) *Japan in the Passing Lane.* Translated by T. Akimoto. New York: Pantheon.

KANTER, R. M. (1977) *Men and Women of the Corporation.* New York: Basic Books.

KAPFERER, B. (1972) *Strategy and Transaction in an African Factory.* Manchester, UK: Manchester University Press.

KIECOLT, K. J., and NATHAN, L. E. (1985) *Secondary Analysis of Survey Data.* Quantitative Applications in the Social Sciences, 53. Newbury Park, CA: Sage.

KUNDA, G. (1992) *Engineering Culture.* Philadelphia, PA: Temple University Press.

LADURIE, E. L. R. (1974) *Peasants of Languedoc.* Translated by J. Day. Urbana: University of Illinois Press.

LAGACE, R. O. (1974) *Nature and Use of the HRAF Files.* New Haven, CT: Human Relations Area Files.

LAND, K. C., and DEANE, G. (1992) "On the large-sample estimation of regression models with spatial- or network-effects terms," in P. V. Marsden (ed.), *Sociological Methodology,* pp. 221-248. Washington, DC: American Sociological Association.

LENDLER, M. (1997) *Crisis and Political Beliefs: The Case of the Colt Firearms Strike.* New Haven, CT: Yale University Press.

LEVINSON, D. (1989) "The Human Relations Area Files." *Reference Services Review* 17: 83-90.

LEVINSON, D., and MALONE, M. (1980) *Toward Explaining Human Culture.* New Haven, CT: Human Relations Areas Files.

LIEBERSON, S. (1991) "Small *N*'s and big conclusions." *Social Forces* 70: 307-320.

LIJPHART, A., and CREPAZ, M. L. (1991) "Corporatism and consensus democracy in 18 countries." *British Journal of Political Science* 21: 345-356.

LINHART, R. (1981) *The Assembly Line.* Translated by M. Crosland. Amherst: University of Massachusetts Press.

LIPSET, S. M., TROW, M. A., and COLEMAN, J. S. (1956) *Union Democracy.* Glencoe, IL: Free Press.

LOCKRIDGE, K. A. (1970) *A New England Town.* New York: Norton.

LOFLAND, J. (1995) "Analytic ethnography." *Journal of Contemporary Ethnography* 24: 30-67.

MacFARLANE, A. (1977) *The Family Life of Ralph Josselin.* New York: Norton.

McCARTHY, J. D., McPHAIL, C., and SMITH, J. (1996) "Images of protest." *American Sociological Review* 61: 478-499.

McIVER, J. P., and CARMINES, E. G. (1981) *Unidimensional Scaling.* Quantitative Applications in the Social Sciences, 24. Beverly Hills, CA: Sage.

McMICHAEL, P. (1990) "Incorporating comparison within a world-historical perspective." *American Sociological Review* 55: 385-397.

MILLS, C. W. (1959) *The Sociological Imagination.* Oxford, UK: Oxford University Press.

MOONEY, C. Z., and DUVAL, R. D. (1993) *Bootstrapping: A Nonparametric Approach to Statistical Inference*. Quantitative Applications in the Social Sciences, 95. Newbury Park, CA: Sage.

MORRILL, C., and FINE, G. A. (1997) "Ethnographic contributions to organizational sociology." *Sociological Methods and Research* 25: 424-451.

MOSTELLER, F., and TUKEY, J. W. (1977) *Data Analysis and Regression*. Reading, MA: Addison-Wesley.

MUELLER, C. (1997) "International press coverage of East German protest events, 1989." *American Sociological Review* 62: 820-832.

MUNROE, R. L., and MUNROE, R. H. (1991) "Comparable field studies." *Behavior Science Research* 25: 155-185.

NAROLL, R. (1960) *Data Quality Control*. New York: Free Press.

NAROLL, R., MICHIK, G. L., and NAROLL, F. (1980) "Holocultural research methods," in H. C. Triandis and J. W. Berry (eds.), *Handbook of Cross-Cultural Research: Vol. 2. Methodology*, pp. 479-521. Boston: Allyn & Bacon.

NOBLIT, G. W., and HARE, R. D. (1988) *Meta-Ethnography: Synthesizing Qualitative Studies*. Qualitative Research Methods Series, 11. Newbury Park, CA: Sage.

O'BRIEN, D. M. (1997) *Judges on Judging*. Chatham, NJ: Chatham House.

OLZAK, S. (1989) "Analysis of events in the study of collective action," in W. R. Scott and J. Blake (eds.), *Annual Review of Sociology*, pp. 119-141. Palo Alto, CA: Annual Reviews.

ORBACH, M. (1977) *Hunters, Seamen and Entrepreneurs*. Berkeley: University of California Press.

OYEN, E. (1990) *Comparative Methodology*. Newbury Park, CA: Sage.

PERRUCCI, R., and STOHL, C. (1997) "Economic restructuring and changing corporate-worker-community relations," in R. Hodson (ed.), *Research in the Sociology of Work: Vol. 6. The Globalization of Work*, pp. 177-195. Greenwich, CT: JAI.

PIERCE, J. L. (1995) *Gender Trials: Emotional Lives in Contemporary Law Firms*. Berkeley: University of California Press.

PLUMMER, K. (1983) *Documents of Life*. London: Allen & Unwin.

PRATT, M. G., and RAFAELI, A. (1997) "Organizational dress as a symbol of multi-layered social identities." *Academy of Management Journal* 40: 862-898.

RAGIN, C. (1987) *The Comparative Method*. Berkeley: University of California Press.

RAGIN, C., and BECKER, H. (eds.) (1992) *What Is a Case?* Cambridge, UK: Cambridge University Press.

RAGIN, C., MAYER, S. E., and DRASS, K. A. (1984) "Assessing discrimination: A Boolean approach." *American Sociological Review* 49: 221-234.

RICHARDS, T. J., and RICHARDS, L. (1994) "Using computers in qualitative research," in N. K. Denzin and Y. S. Lincoln (eds.), *Handbook of Qualitative Research*, pp. 445-462. Thousand Oaks, CA: Sage.

ROETHLISBERGER, F. J., and DICKSON, W. J. (1939) *Management and the Worker*. Cambridge, MA: Harvard University Press.

ROTH, R. (1992) "Is history a process?" *Social Science History* 16: 197-243.

ROTHWAX, H. (1996) *Guilty: The Collapse of Criminal Justice*. New York: Random House.

ROY, D. (1954) "Efficiency and 'the fix': Informal intergroup relations in a piecework machine shop." *American Journal of Sociology* 60: 255-266.

RUBIN, D. B. (1987) *Multiple Imputation for Nonresponse in Surveys.* New York: John Wiley.

SCHWARTZMAN, H. B. (1993) *Ethnography in Organizations.* Qualitative Research Methods Series, 27. Newbury Park, CA: Sage.

SHAPIRO, G., and MARKOFF, J. (1997) *Revolutionary Demands: A Content Analysis of the Cahiers de Doleances of 1789.* Stanford, CA: Stanford University Press.

SHAW, C. R. (1951) *The Jackroller.* Chicago: University of Chicago Press.

SILVER, B. J. (1995) "Labor unrest and world-systems analysis." *Review* 18: 7-34.

SINGLETON, R. A., JR., STRAITS, B. C., and STRAITS, M. M. (1993) *Approaches to Social Research.* 2nd ed. New York: Oxford University Press.

SLAYTON, R. A. (1986) *Back of the Yards.* Chicago: University of Chicago Press.

SMITH, V. (1990) *Managing in the Corporate Interest.* Berkeley: University of California Press.

SMITH, V. (In press) "Ethnographies of work and the work of ethnographer," in P. Atkinson, A. Coffey, S. Delamont, L. Lofland, and J. Lofland (eds.), *Handbook of Ethnography.* Thousand Oaks, CA: Sage.

SPRADLEY, J. P., and MANN, B. J. (1975) *The Cocktail Waitress.* New York: John Wiley.

STEPAN-NORRIS, J., and ZEITLIN, M. (1995) "Union democracy, radical leadership, and the hegemony of capital." *American Sociological Review* 60: 829-850.

STEVENS, J. (1997) "Ideology and social structure." *Comparative Studies in Society and History* 39: 401-409.

STONE, L. (1979) "The revival of narrative." *Past and Present* 85: 3-24.

STRAUSS, A., and J. CORBIN (1990) *Basics of Qualitative Research.* Newbury Park, CA: Sage.

STRYKER, R. (1996) "Beyond history versus theory: Strategic narrative and sociological explanation." *Sociological Methods and Research* 23: 304-352.

TAYLOR, C. L., and JODICE, D. A. (1983) *World Handbook of Political and Social Indicators.* New Haven, CT: Yale University Press.

THORNTON, J. M. (1978) *Politics and Power in a Slave Society.* Baton Rouge: Louisiana State University Press.

TILLY, C. (1981) *As Sociology Meets History.* New York: Academic Press.

TOBIN, J. (1990) "The HRAF as radical text?" *Cultural Anthropology* 5: 473-487.

TRICE, H. H., and BEYER, J. M. (1992) *The Cultures of Work Organizations.* Englewood Cliffs, NJ: Prentice Hall.

TURNER, S. (1980) *Night Shift in a Pickle Factory.* San Pedro, CA: Singlejack.

VALLAS, S. P. (1987) "The labor process as a source of class consciousness." *Sociological Forum* 2: 251-273.

VECSEY, G. (1974) *One Sunset a Week.* New York: Dutton.

WALKER, C. R., and GUEST, R. H. (1952) *The Man on the Assembly Line.* Cambridge, MA: Harvard University Press.

WALTON, J. (1992) "Making the theoretical case," in C. Ragin and H. Becker (eds.), *What Is a Case?,* pp. 121-137. Cambridge, UK: Cambridge University Press.

WEBER, R. P. (1990) *Basic Content Analysis.* 2nd ed., Quantitative Applications in the Social Sciences, 49. Newbury Park, CA: Sage.

WELSH, S. (1994) "Cultures of harassment in the workplace." Dissertation, Department of Sociology, Indiana University.

WESTWOOD, S. (1982) *All Day, Every Day.* London: Pluto Press.

WOLF, F. M. (1986) *Meta-Analysis*. Quantitative Applications in the Social Sciences, 59. Beverly Hills, CA: Sage.

ZETKA, J. R., JR. (1992) "Work organization and wildcat strikes in the U.S. auto industry." *American Sociological Review* 57: 214-226.

ZETKA, J. R., JR., and WALSH, J. P. (1994) "A qualitative protocol for studying technological change in the labor process." *Bulletin de Methodologie Sociologique* 45: 37-73.

ABOUT THE AUTHOR

RANDY HODSON is Professor of Sociology at The Ohio State University. Previously, he taught at the University of Texas–Austin and Indiana University–Bloomington. He is the editor of the JAI Press annual series on *Research in the Sociology of Work.* He is the coauthor with Teresa A. Sullivan of *The Social Organization of Work* (2nd ed., 1995) and the author of *Working With Dignity* (forthcoming). In addition to conducting workplace studies, he also studies international social and political issues, with a focus on the states of the former Yugoslavia. His research has been supported by the National Science Foundation, the Department of Labor, the National Council for Eurasian and East European Research, and the International Research and Exchanges Board. He is the author of more than 50 articles that have appeared in scholarly journals such as the *American Sociological Review,* the *American Journal of Sociology, Social Forces, Human Relations,* and *Work and Occupations.* He received his Ph.D. from the University of Wisconsin.